The MISSIONARY DISCIPLE

Going and Growing

Dr. Jacob Youmans

Tri-Pillar Publishing

THE MISSIONARY DISCIPLE

Copyright © 2019 by Jacob Youmans

Tri-Pillar Publishing
Anaheim Hills, California
Website: www.TriPillarPublishing.com
Email: tripillarpublishing@cox.net

ALL RIGHTS RESERVED. This book or parts thereof may not be reproduced in any form without prior written permission of the publisher.

International Standard Book Number: 978-1-942654-04-9

Library of Congress Control Number: 2019943275

Scriptures taken from the Holy Bible, New International Version®, NIV®. Copyright ©1973, 1978, 1984, 2011 by Biblica, Inc.™ Used by permission of Zondervan. All rights reserved worldwide. www.zondervan.com The "NIV" and "New International Version" are trademarks registered in the United States Patent and Trademark Office by Biblica, Inc.™

First edition, June, 2019

Printed in the United States of America

To Dr. Jim McConnell, boss, mentor, and friend: You started the Director of Christian Education Program at Concordia University Texas in 1999, and you insisted that it be "different." You did not necessarily use the term "Missionary Disciple," but you modeled it. Thank you! Enjoy your "real" retirement.

Contents

Acknowledgments   7

Foreword by Dr. Grant Carey   9

What in the World Is a Missionary Disciple?!?   13

How to Use This Book   19

Chapter 1 – The Identity Questions   21
    Who Are You?   21
    Imagine Your Image   30

Chapter 2 – C: Corporate Worship   39
    Who's Who in Worship   39
    Jesus Was No Pew Potato!   44
    Ideas for You to Investigate
        Finding Your Sanctuary   52
        Come and See!   57
        The Sacred Experienced   61
        Don't Just Sit There…   67

Chapter 3 – S: Small Group   71
    Good Things Come in Small Packages   71
    The Ultimate Small-Group Leader   76
    Ideas for You to Investigate
        Gather Around the Word!   82
        Serving Side by Side   86

Stronger Together	90
Partners in Prayer	93
Chapter 4 – I: Individual	**99**
All by Myself… with Jesus	99
Keep Watch!	103
How's Your Spiritual Health?	108
Ideas for You to Investigate	
Eating the Scroll	116
Writing Loudly	120
When and Where for Prayer	125
Posture Matters	130
Go Away!	133
Chapter 5 – Going as We're Growing	**141**
Chapter 6 – Not a Tame God	**149**
Brief Autobiography	**153**
Endnotes & Additional Resources	**155**

Acknowledgments

To Jesus: Thank You for calling me to be a disciple on mission! Life has certainly never been boring! Thanks for giving me all of these coworkers in the kingdom!
- To Dr. Grant Carey: I am so honored that you would write the Foreword for *The Missionary Disciple*! You are such a blessing to our students, and to me! You are an absolute joy to work with, and while they say that no one is irreplaceable, you sure make me question that adage! And I cannot wait until we get to celebrate that Dodgers World Series championship – this year, right?!
- To all past, present, and future Concordia Texas DCE students: Thank you for entrusting your training to us! I hope and pray that this book will bless you on your journey, now and when you are teaching future Missionary Disciples.
- To Peter Dibble: I don't know how you do it! The depth and meaning behind your images and designs are more powerful than most people will initially understand. Readers, please be sure to re-examine the cover after every chapter or so! Thank you!
- To Josephine and Andy Dibble and the Tri-Pillar family: "Thank you" seems too small! This is book #5. How did we come this far? Your patience, encouragement, and brutal honesty have formed me as a writer/speaker/teacher/minister. I'm so excited to see what our next project(s) will be! Thank you!

- To my parents, Kim and Sandra Youmans, who discipled me and sent me on a mission from day 1: Thanks for modeling all of this for me!
- To our daughters, Maile and Leilani: During the course of writing this book, you both got confirmed. And how funny is it that God worked it out where I actually got to confirm both of you. That was one of the greatest honors of my life – to watch you boldly and publicly confess your desire to be Missionary Disciples! I am so proud of you and excited to see what God has in store for you!
- To my amazing wife, Christy: You really personify this "going and growing" idea. You are one of the best evangelists I know! On many occasions I have been sitting in church, looking around, and realizing that most of the people present are there because you invited them! There is no one I would rather "go and grow" old with! Oh – and, I know you hate the cold, but can we please go visit Antarctica?

God – Father, Son, and Holy Spirit: Thank You for calling us to go and grow! May all come to know You as LORD!

Foreword

A healthy Christian life cannot be stitched together from a series of disjointed mountain-top experiences. We need a Christian spirituality that endures the shadowy, low-lying valleys and the rocky slopes in between all those glorious summits.
Andrew Byers, *Faith Without Illusions*[1]

Growing up as a teenager in Southern California, my spiritual life was a lot like Tarzan, the famous orphaned Disney character brought up in the wilderness. Now to be clear, I was not raised by apes, but I did tend to swing from branch to branch – only in my life, the branches were spiritual mountain-top experiences. Camp, retreats, youth gatherings, and lock-ins: these were my branches. They kept my faith afloat and I would look forward to the next one as soon as the glow wore off from the previous experience. This type of spiritual growth was all I knew and it sustained me for a few years. However, there came a point where I wanted, no, *needed* more. At this point in my life, I had a pastor and some other key spiritual mentors who introduced me to spiritual practices and disciplines. These daily, weekly, and monthly disciplines gave my faith new life and revealed to me that mountaintop experiences were good, but no longer the only source of my once-spotty spiritual growth.

I have learned many lessons about spiritual growth over the years, and many of them are contained in this book – a resource

I wish I had access to several decades ago! What is so fun about the material found in the following pages is that I have had a front-row seat witnessing Jake Youmans live these practices out in his daily life. The man has literally worshiped in churches on every continent (except Antarctica... but I believe he will get there one day soon!). Jake has been part of every type of small group imaginable: in houses, churches, bars, under trees in Africa, and even at the base of the Egyptian pyramids. I have also witnessed him devote time to being in the Word and with God, whether on an airplane, on a walk, or during breakfast. His wisdom and experience with spiritual growth is something I take note of, and often try to emulate in my own life.

The game of baseball is one of the many things Jake and I have in common. We love to watch it and have taken in many games together. Additionally, being diehard fans of the Los Angeles Dodgers has given us some major shared highs and lows over the past few years. There is nothing quite like being at a game surrounded by the sights of beautiful grass, sounds of cheers, and smells of food wafting through the air. However, I believe the best thing about baseball is the strategy and teamwork involved. You never know what will happen, and rarely can one person win the game on their own. Baseball is a fantastic metaphor for our spiritual life, where the unexpected inevitably comes and you can't go at it alone. Over the past seven years, I have had the privilege to work alongside Jake in a team environment. We may not come close to emulating the greatness of the Dodgers, but we are able to lift one another up and challenge each other when it comes to our spiritual lives. We have gone through hard and unexpected times, but our faith and daily practices have kept us going – knowing that Jesus is ultimately in control. Without these C.S.I. practices in our lives, I am not sure where we would be today.

As I look back to my spiritual upbringing, I would have loved to have something like Jake's C.S.I. model outlined here in the pages to come! To have the wisdom of sustainable spiritual growth would have been refreshing and challenging in some of my "angsty" teenage years. Spiritual growth has always been encouraged by leaders and churches, but Jake helps us see it in a well-organized way of living. The quote by Andrew Byers at the beginning of this Foreword reminds us that we need a faith which will help us celebrate the good we see in life, but also everyday faith which can carry us through the "shadowy, low-lying valleys and the rocky slopes" that life often brings us. A Missionary Disciple will inevitably have challenges, and needs the spiritual food that the C.S.I. model offers.

May you be blessed by Jake's work, which has been brought about by so many years of trials, patience, and ultimately, growth. I challenge you to reflect seriously on the questions at the end of each section and to push yourself to engage in the challenges. Spiritual growth is messy and there is no perfect system. Give yourself the grace to fail at times, but also find that friend who will challenge you as you embark upon this exciting journey of growing closer to Jesus and His heart to form you more like Him.

And, may your faith be less like Tarzan, and more like that of a diehard baseball fan whose team will one day win the World Series.

Dr. Grant Carey
Associate DCE Program Director, Concordia University Texas
Austin, Texas

What in the World Is a Missionary Disciple?!?

The Missionary Disciple. I wrestled more with the title of this book than the previous four books combined. It took me a while – but now I love it! Here's why: I hope and pray that after reading this book you will see the title, *The Missionary Disciple,* as redundant.

I feel a tension in the church. In my current role of training, mentoring, and placing church workers across the planet, I have the honor and privilege of visiting about 40 churches a year. The tension comes from a perceived paradox. Considering how many paradoxes we celebrate – from saint/sinner, to life out of death, to 1 plus 1 equaling 1 in Christian marriage math – you'd think that we would be OK with tension.

I'm not talking about the worship wars or even necessarily doctrinal differences; the tension I feel most in the church is one between discipleship and missions. There are some who believe that the role of the church is to care for the flock, and others who argue that the church exists for those who are not part of the flock yet. Have you felt this tension?

As with so many examples of tension, this is actually a good thing. Don't let this tension frustrate or concern you. The church needs to be for those here *and* for those not yet here. But first, let's define these words "discipleship" and "missions."

- *Disciples* who are following Jesus will naturally have a passion for the lost, because Jesus had a passion for the lost – which is defined as missions

- *Missions* is about connecting people to Jesus, and to do so effectively, a missionary has to be in a growing faith relationship with Jesus – which is defined as discipleship

The Great Commandment (Matthew 22:36-40) and The Great Commission (Matthew 28:16-20) need to be taught hand in hand. When they are not, both lose their depth and power. Christians are called to use The Great Commandment (Love the Lord and Neighbor) to fulfill The Great Commission (Take the Gospel to the World). A fascinating thing happens when you take the Gospel to the world; it increases your desire to love your neighbor. Loving your neighbor is a witness to the world, and loving the world is a witness to your neighbor.

Missions is about going – down the street or around the world. Missionaries *go*. Discipleship is about growing – growing in your identity, mission, and purpose in following Jesus. Disciples *grow*. Going helps you grow, and growing helps you go. The more you experience Jesus through missions, the more you grow in Him. The more you grow in Him, the more you desire to go – serving and telling others about Him.

Growing and going may sound simple, but make no mistake: Truly growing brings pain. I remember as a child experiencing intense pain in my legs. We went to the doctor and he said it was just normal "growing pains." Evidently, growing pains are more than an 80s sitcom!

Going is exhausting. Going brings a lack of sleep, skipping meals, and sometimes is very expensive. Going exposes you to new illnesses and diseases. When you go, you may get lost.

When you go, you may get taken advantage of. Pain just might be the only thing that growing and going have in common!

Speaking of painful: Did you see *Batman v Superman*? It is not a very good movie. I wanted so badly to like it! While much has been theorized as to why it doesn't work, I believe it all comes down to the "v." The movie plays Batman *against* Superman. The filmmakers, in an effort to be provocative, created an unnecessary tension. But Batman and Superman need each other. They do their best work together. They are both good guys, for goodness' sake!

Having written extensively on missions in my previous books, I want to refocus the lens a bit and attempt to view missions through the lens of discipleship. Missionaries are disciples, and disciples can't help but be missionaries. Missionaries and disciples are both good guys, for goodness' sake!

A key to really understanding discipleship and missions is discipline. Unless you're a Marine, this might be one of the more discouraging/frustrating words in the English language. When hearing that word, some of you will think about the discipline you received as a kid from your parents, teacher, coach, or other key authority figure. Some will think back to a firm lecture where you were told that you needed to be more "disciplined."

When it comes to a biblical view on discipline, one of the most frequently-paraphrased Bible verses is from Solomon's Proverbs: *Spare the rod, spoil the child.* Proverbs 13:24 has been used to support everything from spanking kids to the death penalty. However, when we use this verse alone, we do not realize the true meaning of the proverb. The word "rod" used here is the same word used in the 23rd Psalm, where we are told that the Good Shepherd's *rod and staff comfort me*.

Discipline is meant to provide comfort! Discipline is about learning and growing! This word is also the root of the word "discipleship." To be a disciple of Jesus requires discipline… a discipline that is a comfort and provides peace, hope, and love! And discipline is required to share that peace, hope, and love with a hurting world. Discipleship is missions. The call to follow Jesus is to be a Missionary Disciple.

Wherever you are in your journey of following Jesus, I hope this book will help you process and explore some ancient concepts of spiritual disciplines as we seek to follow and serve Jesus in our modern world. In my experience, when we find our identity in Him, we want to grow closer to Him, and we desire to tell others about Him – but we just don't always know how. I hope and pray that this little book will answer some of the "how" questions. I promise there will be no rocket science in this book – but it will require some discipline to be a disciple and missionary.

I love working with college freshmen! Many of them are experiencing freedom for the first time. It's always fun to watch them realize that they can actually go to the movies on a school night! With this newfound freedom comes a need for personal discipline. Just because you *could* doesn't mean you *should*. As much as those of us who are older might like to think that we have grown and matured a lot since we were college freshmen, aren't we always wrestling with freedom and discipline? It's a lifelong journey of discovery.

I'll be praying for you as you investigate what it means for you personally to be a disciple of and missionary for Jesus!

Perhaps someday, everyone will view "Missionary Disciple" as redundant. Like Jewish rabbi – I mean, how many rabbis do you know who aren't Jewish? I have no doubt that God will bless your investigation as you experience Him working in you and through you!

How to Use This Book

I hope you are able to do more than just read through this book. This book will require some commitment. I encourage you to *actively* read it. Highlight, circle, and underline words and phrases that are meaningful to you. Have a Bible (or a Bible app on your phone) next to you to look up references and the context for the quoted verses. This might not be a book to try and read all in one sitting. Process it. Think through it. To help you with this, I have included two key sections.

- First, there are "investigative questions" at the end of each section. Given them some thought. Answer them honestly. Notice the space given at the end of each question. Write in that space, and use it to process, think, and dream. Reading and writing will exponentially help you to retain the information and allow you to work toward permanent life change. Ask other people the questions as well. Don't just glance over the questions – take the time to really work through them. Let them help you *grow*.
- Second, the "action items" at the end of each section were carefully chosen to help you put the key concepts of the book into practice. Try them. Some will be easier, and some will be more challenging. Again, don't just read them. In fact, all of them will require you to put the book down and go do something. Let them help you *go*.

In addition, make sure to read the Endnotes & Additional Resources section at the end of the book. Besides citing my sources, I provide that section to help refer you to resources, websites, and additional information that will aid you on your Missionary Disciple journey.

Above all, pray as you read this book. Ask God to open your eyes and your heart, and to help you grow in the areas where you may need strengthening. Pray that He will not only help you grow, but that He will embolden you to GO – to serve others and share His love.

Now I should prepare you up front that to actually do all of this will be challenging. It will also be time-consuming. Some people you talk to about it will just not understand. But can you think of anything in life that is really worth doing that isn't hard? It's similar to lifting weights. Your muscles are broken down, which is painful – but then rebuild to be stronger. I pray this book builds you up and makes you stronger. And speaking of lifting weights, it can be very easy to "cheat" yourself while lifting. You could not do the full extension. You could use less weight. You could "fudge" the count. But to truly get the most benefits from the workout, you have to fully commit. If it's worth doing, it's worth doing *right*. I hope and pray you are able to fully commit to this book and follow through.

The book *TransforMission,* by Michael Wilder and Shane Parker, researched the value of short-term mission trips. Essentially, what they discovered is that short-term missions is life changing when it becomes long-term missions. It's all about commitment to change. "Comprehensive follow-through provides an environment for commitment to mission to be established and animated for long-term devotion."[1] I pray this book provides that environment for you.

May God bless you as you explore Missionary Discipleship!

Chapter 1

The Identity Questions

Who Are You?

Who are you? This is an important question. It's only three words, which makes it a fun paradox of simple and complex. Can you picture the caterpillar in *Alice in Wonderland* blowing smoke all over sweet little Alice as he asks this question again and again?[1] This book might end up being just like that smoking caterpillar!

In his book, *Organic Church: Growing Faith Where Life Happens*, missiologist Neil Cole writes, "To reach the world for Christ today we have to sit in the smoking section. That is where lost people are found, and if you make them put their cigarette out to hear the message they will be thinking about only one thing: 'When can I get another cigarette?'"[2] That means we are going to be a little uncomfortable and experience more than a few "coughs" along the way. I should warn you now that I do hope my book makes you a little uncomfortable. It is designed to be challenging – asking you to live in the tension – and hopefully it will make you think differently. It has certainly been convicting and challenging for me to write! Notice too that Dr. Cole doesn't say we are to "smoke" in the "smoking section." We're called to be there with them, not smoke. We're called to integrity and transparency. But we will not sacrifice integrity for transparency. Speaking of transparency, we are going to get *very* personal – and it all starts with that all-important question: *Who are you?*

This might be more than just an important question. It might be *the* question. If truly examined and answered honestly, this question becomes a differently-worded twist on those timeless questions: *What is the meaning of life?* and *What is my purpose?* I truly believe that questions are often better than answers, and these two are great questions to ask yourself. However, we need to start with *Who are you?*

*We are created in God's image;
this means that if we don't find our identity in Christ,
we will never find it anywhere*

I wonder if many of us just gloss over the deeper meaning behind the question *Who are you?* and simply state our name and perhaps our occupation or place of residence. Historically, people's identities were often tied to whoever their father or grandfather was. Over time, many of our last names have attempted to answer this identity question. If your last name is Johnson, this means at some point someone in your family had a father named John. If your last name is Shepherd, guess what one of your ancestors did for a living?

But the question *Who are you?* needs to take you much further than just your basic identity. It also has to hit on mission

Chapter 1 – The Identity Questions   23

and purpose. Why are you even here? If the question *Who are you?* doesn't scare you, the question *Why are you here?* surely will! Our identity, mission, and purpose go hand in hand. You cannot have one without the others.

CSI: Crime Scene Investigation started its long-running television series in 2000. It was a hit, and quickly became one of those groundbreaking shows that many tried to copy. As of this writing, there have been four legitimate manifestations of the *CSI* franchise: *CSI, CSI: Miami, CSI: NY,* and *CSI: Cyber*.[3] And next time you are in Las Vegas, you can even pretend to be a real-life crime scene investigator at the MGM Grand® hotel, through *CSI: The Experience*.

At its core, *CSI* is a typical "whodunit" cop show. The major difference, however, is in the perspective. *CSI* was the first show on television to come from the perspective of the forensics unit. Forensics involves the use of science and technology to investigate clues and establish facts. It is both an art and a science… and interestingly enough, so is being a follower of Jesus! In both cases, there needs to be a consideration of both tangible evidence and following one's "gut" or intuition – a harmony of thinking and feeling. "Now faith is confidence in what we hope for and assurance about what we do not see" (Hebrews 11:1).

Before this show ever aired, many people didn't even know that a crime scene investigator (C.S.I.) is an actual job within police departments. A friend of mine who used to work as a C.S.I. told me that after the show came out, a job opening in his department that would have previously had a dozen or so applicants now has over 200! There have even been major issues with jurors since the *CSI* shows became popular, because they expect every case to have as complete evidence as the C.S.I. team gathered on television. Unfortunately, that's just not the reality in most cases. The show is certainly making an impression on people!

On the show, C.S.I.s help solve weekly mysteries by investigating evidence and searching for the truth. And they do this all under the melodic sounds of The Who's musical question – "Who Are You." If you are unfamiliar with the song, the chorus is simple:

> *Who are you?*
> *Who, who, who, who?*
> *Who are you?*
> *Who, who, who, who?*[4]

Just three little words and only one punctuation mark. As I said earlier, it's a paradox of simple and complex – like so many things in life. There are certainly quick and easy answers to the question, but they only satisfy for so long. *Who are you?*

Several years ago, after I had just finished a speaking engagement, I wandered to the back of the auditorium where an elderly gentleman flashed me a huge smile. I immediately came over to him to say hello. He reached out his hand to me and asked: "Who are you?"

"I am the speaker you just heard," I replied, not quite sure where he was going with this question.

"Right! But who are you?" he asked again, smiling even bigger than before.

"That's a complicated question," I answered, and he nodded, apparently satisfied with my response. Who we are isn't easily defined by our name and occupation! (Or, for those of you in college, your name and major. Your major is *not* who you are!) What we do isn't who we are – but what we do should be a basic clue as to who we are. Mission should lead to meaning.

In the movie *Anger Management,* with Adam Sandler and Jack Nicholson, we get to see the strange but (spoiler alert!) eventually effective techniques of Jack Nicholson's character (Dr. Buddy Rydell) as he tries to help Adam Sandler's character (Dave Buznik) overcome his anger issues. Dave doesn't believe that he has an anger problem, but is attending anger management classes to make his girlfriend happy. During their first group meeting, the "Who are you?" question stumps a confused Dave:

Dr. Buddy Rydell: "So, Dave. Tell us about yourself. Who are you?"

Dave Buznik: "Well, I'm an executive assistant for a major pet products company."

Dr. Buddy Rydell: *[interrupts him]* "Dave, I don't want you to tell us what you *do*. I want you to tell us who you *are*."

Dave Buznik: "Oh, alright, um... I'm a pretty good guy. I like playing tennis on occasion."

Dr. Buddy Rydell: "Also, not your hobbies Dave. Just tell us who you are."

Dave Buznik: *[stumped]* "Maybe you could give me an example of what a good answer would be? Um... *[to Lou]* What did you say?"

[The group laughs]

Dr. Buddy Rydell: "You want Lou to tell you who you are?"

Dave Buznik: "No, I just, uh... I'm a nice, easygoing man, I might be a little indecisive at times..."

Dr. Buddy Rydell: "Dave, you're describing your personality. I just want to know... who you are."

Dave Buznik: *[snaps]* "I don't know what the hell you want me to say!"[5]

Maybe this question is more complex than it seems! Now, please don't snap at me as I ask *you* this same question! *Who are you?* might feel like a loaded question sometimes – especially for a follower of Jesus. Our identity is found in Jesus. The Sunday School answer to the question of our identity is, "I am a Christian." But what does that mean, exactly?

The word *Christian* literally means "follower of Christ," or "little Christ." The word *Christ* is a title meaning "Anointed One." It's actually a Greek word; the Hebrew word with the same meaning is the word *Messiah*. So when you say you are a Christian, you are saying that you follow an anointed person – which is a good answer, especially when one considers the command of Jesus to the first disciples: "Follow me" (Matthew 4:19). With so much talk of leadership in our world today, it is very important to start our discussion on identity, mission, and purpose with the concept of *followership*. Missions and discipleship, going and growing, all start with "followership."

One of my favorite classes to teach is a course called Leadership Development. Every semester, on the first day of class, I open up with the line, "I wish I could call this course

Followership Development – but if I did, I'd be afraid that no one would sign up for it!" As Christians, our identity, mission, and purpose are formed as we follow Jesus Christ, the Anointed One, step by step.

Let's look at the history of the word *Christian* for a bit. Would you believe that it's only used in the Bible three times? Two of those occurrences are found in the book of Acts. It's used in chapter 11, verse 26 when we are told, "The disciples were called Christians first at Antioch." Think about that – the term wasn't even used until eleven chapters into the book of Acts! It also wasn't used first to describe the apostles or any of the "famous" Jesus followers. It was used to describe random, unnamed people in Antioch who were living their faith.

We see the word *Christian* used again later in Acts – chapter 26, verse 28 – when St. Paul is on trial. He shares his personal story with King Agrippa, and the king responds with, "Do you think that in such a short time you can persuade me to be a Christian?" St Paul's response: "Short time or long – I pray to God that not only you but all who are listening to me today may become what I am, except for these chains" (Acts 26:29). Missionary Paul knows that his chains are a part of following Jesus. He wishes it was not like this, at least for others, but he knows it is. The life of the follower of Jesus is one of persecution.

Peter picks up this same persecution theme in 1 Peter 4:16: "If you suffer as a Christian, do not be ashamed, but praise God that you bear that name." *Praise God that we bear that name!* Even through the suffering, pain, and realities of this life – through the constant growing and going – we praise God that we have Jesus' name written on us! Our identity, mission, and purpose are absolutely formed in Jesus.

So the new question for us then becomes: *How do we form our identity, mission, and purpose in Jesus?* The answer to that question will lead to the answer of *Who are you?* Genesis chapter 1 says that we are created in God's image; this means that if we don't find our identity in Christ, we will never find it anywhere. Just as a C.S.I. searches for truth, the follower of Jesus clings to the words of Jesus: "I am the way and the truth and the life" (John 14:6). As Christians, we may not have all the answers, but we have the *truth!* And as Jesus says, "The truth will set you free" (John 8:32). Did you catch the mission concept in there too? Once we have the truth – God will use us to help others become free! Disciples are on a mission of freedom!

Investigative Questions:

1) When people ask, "Who are you?" how do you usually respond? Why?

2) Do you think "Who are you?" is a simple or complex question? Explain.

3) How do you think identity, mission, and purpose are connected?

4) What does being a Christian mean to you?

5) What is the difference between *truth* and *answers*?

6) What does it mean to be a follower?

7) What do you feel you need to investigate about yourself?

Action Item:

Choose five Christian friends or acquaintances and ask each of them: "What does being a Christian mean to you?" How are their answers similar and different? How do their answers compare and contrast to your answer?

Imagine Your Image

Creation is God's imagination on full display! It's a creative creation that paradoxes the simple and complex. And YOU are the top of creation! As we explore such ideas as identity, mission, and purpose, the best place to start is with the Creator's original intent. Why were human beings created in the first place? What was God's original intent and design for us?

No one knows the creation like the Creator! "So God created mankind in his own image, in the image of God he created them; male and female he created them" (Genesis 1:27). The word "image" has confused people and caused more than a few good theological debates for thousands of years. This image idea is not as simple as looking in a mirror. And doesn't it sound arrogant to say that we are created in God's image? What does it really mean? *The Message*, Eugene Peterson's paraphrase of the Bible, says that God created people to be "godlike."[1] Other translations use the word likeness. The Latin phrase is *imago Dei*, which means image, shadow, or likeness of God.

The first important thing to grasp from all of this is that human beings are created in God's image, and not in the image of any other created thing or being. While our DNA is 99% the same as a chimpanzee[2] – and according to the Genesis creation account, apes were created first – we are *not* created in their image!

Some people focus on the fact that we are created to be perfect, just as God is perfect. And while this is certainly true, the sad reality is that our sinful rebellion has caused us to lose that perfection. Satan gets the image idea – in fact, he took on the image of an animal to confuse and tempt those who were created in the image of God. The loss of perfection is a direct result of sin. Death and decay are now our image (Genesis 3). It is so painful to watch a loved one die. The human body decays in very ugly ways.

While many of us live in fear of having our identity stolen, Satan is the ultimate identity thief – he's an "image thief"! He stole our identity in the Garden of Eden, and he still tries to rob us of our identity in Christ today!

To restore our identity, God took on the image of man. As we read in John 1:14, "The Word became flesh and made his dwelling among us." Or as *The Message* puts it, "God moved into the neighborhood."[3] All of this was done to restore and reclaim our image, our identity, and provide us with mission and purpose!

Perhaps a more holistic approach to understanding this idea of image comes from the concept of the Trinity. Now the actual word *trinity* is not found anywhere in the Bible – but the word is commonly used to describe the nature of God. God is three in one: The Father, The Son, and The Holy Spirit. There is one God with three "persons." Each "person" of God has a separate and distinct role and "personality." But when all three are viewed in harmony, you have the true image of God!

Think about the baptism of Jesus – a story found in all three of the synoptic Gospels (Matthew 3:13-17, Mark 1:9-11, Luke 3:21-22). The waters of baptism are laid upon Jesus by John the Baptist. At the same time, there is the voice of God the Father saying, "This is my Son, whom I love; with him I am well pleased" (Matthew 3:17). At the very same time, the Spirit of God descends like a dove upon Jesus. So you have all three persons of God visibly together to create the true image of God.

Or think about the crucifixion of Jesus, which is a story told in all four of the Gospel accounts. The Son of God – True God and True Man who knew no sin – became sin on our behalf. Jesus breathed His last, dying for the sins of the world, and with that final breath the three persons of the Holy Trinity are shown together again. The God of creation responds with darkness over the whole land, and an earthquake that shakes so violently that some of the dead are awakened! Then the Holy Spirit enters the temple of God and rips into two the curtain in the Holy of Holies that was used for generations to separate God and man. At the moment of Jesus' death, we see all three parts of the triune God together to give us the true image of God.

In The Great Commission, found in Matthew 28, Jesus tells His followers to baptize "in the name of the Father and of the Son and of the Holy Spirit" (Matthew 28:19). Baptism is a reminder of all three persons of God together to create the true image of God. Just as the three persons of God were seen together at Jesus' baptism, so they are seen together at every Christian baptism!

Let's view the Trinity through the lens of God's image. What if part of the image of God was a human trinity? When Jesus was asked which is the greatest commandment, He replied, "Love the Lord your God with all your heart and with all your soul and with all your mind" (Matthew 22:37). Our heart, soul, and mind are certainly connected, but they can also act independently of each other. Let's take a closer look at what this means.

Heart: When you hear "heart" you probably think emotional, but when the Hebrews heard the word "heart," it meant the stomach. Heart was more about gut, or the body, rather than the emotional heart used in our modern understanding. Heart is about the physical – the flesh. We all have certain natural, innate, physical reflexes. When the doctor hits us right below the knee, our leg kicks up. Our mind doesn't tell our leg to kick up – the body acts independently. It's a reflex, which literally means an action without conscious thought. Or when you are scared by something, you jump back (or some of you punch it in the face) which is called "fight-or-flight response." You didn't cognitively think, *I should jump back to avoid this life-threatening object.* Your physical instincts just kicked in. Sometimes our body acts independently of the rest of us.

Mind: We've all noticed that there are times when our mind just wanders off on its own. This usually happens without cognitively thinking about it. You may be physically present, but your mind is somewhere else entirely. Some call this daydreaming. It is rather amusing to look into the eyes of students in class and realize that while their body is sitting at that desk, their mind is not siting in that body! (Of course this *never* happens in any of *my* classes – but I hear stories from other professors!) In a research study done in 2012 on car crashes and mind wandering, it is believed that 17% of car accidents were a result of mind wandering.[4] Our mind can go off on its own even when we are doing something as important and potentially deadly as driving a car! Have you ever looked into someone's eyes and realized that they were simply not there? Sometimes our mind acts independently of the rest of us.

Soul: Our soul is the spiritual part of us. There are times when our spirit just soars and takes over our whole self. Maybe it's in a worship service, where a certain song, hymn, prayer, or Scripture passage really connects with us, and the joy in our soul fills all of our senses. Maybe it's on a mission trip, where we are able to do or say things that we didn't think were possible. I love it when I am speaking words of faith to someone but realize that it's not really *me* who's speaking. Maybe it's in a conversation with a non-Christian who is so close to connecting to Jesus Christ as Lord and Savior. Sometimes, for whatever reason, the Holy Spirit just overtakes our soul and leads us into the presence of God and gives us words and abilities that we know are not our own. We didn't necessarily do anything physically or mentally to cause it, but the soul takes over. Just as with the heart and mind, sometimes our soul acts independently from the rest of us.

But the most profound human experiences – the moments when we realize our true humanity, and the idea of God's image – are when all three "parts" of the human trinity come together. We've all witnessed and experienced these moments, but we may not have known how to define them. Perhaps at a baptism. Maybe it was the birth of your child. Maybe it was your wedding day. (Or maybe it was when you consummated your marriage!) Maybe it was at the funeral of a loved one. Maybe it was when someone you were praying for finally connected to Jesus as Lord and Savior. Maybe it was a time you lived out your faith in boldness. When we truly realize who we are in God's image, then we are fully human. Our identity is lost without God.

Satan is the ultimate identity thief

In the chapters ahead, we will be examining the ways through which we connect with Jesus Christ, as well as taking a closer look at the connection we have with our fellow believers and those who are not yet believers. We are going to explore our identity, mission, and purpose through three different elements: **C**orporate worship, **S**mall groups, and **I**ndividual time. These unique and specific connections just happen to make up the acronym **C.S.I.**

To truly find your identity, mission, and purpose in Christ and in life, all three of these three elements need to be working together in harmony. Please note that I will be using the image of harmony rather than "balance." Balance gives us the image of scales and all things being equal. But in music, harmony brings out true beauty and fullness while at the same time maintaining dominant tones and melodies that are prioritized at different times and in different ways. That's also the way our life in Christ should be!

This book will not reveal any big secrets or shortcuts. I will be outlining different ways of practicing the spiritual disciplines within these three elements, specifically reading the Word, having an active prayer life, and attending worship services. Most likely you have already participated in one or more of these. (Even if you haven't experienced any of them yet, please keep reading!) All three are essential for wholeness and to realize our full potential as a follower of Jesus. When all three are together, we can fully live in the tension of discipleship and missions. When all three are in harmony, we find our identity, mission, and purpose in Christ.

For example, Christians who just attend worship on Sunday mornings but don't think about God's Word the rest of the week are compartmentalizing their faith and not allowing it to permeate into the other six days of their week. Other people may only be involved in small groups – usually with people who look, act, and think very similarly to them. But by not attending corporate worship, they have no sense of the larger Body of Christ. This, too, leaves us incomplete. And still others think that they only need to connect with God one-on-one, on their own, and can ignore the people around them. This could not be further from the truth! Dietrich Bonhoeffer was a pastor in Germany during World War II. He ran an underground seminary and was defiant to the Nazi regime. In his book, *Life Together*, he says, "Let him who cannot be alone beware of community." Then a few sentences later, he says the opposite is true as well: "Let him who is not in community beware of being alone."[5] We need both!

When the different parts of C.S.I. – corporate, small group, and individual – are all active in our lives, we experience wholeness like never before! You will be a Missionary Disciple! Now that we've explored our image, let's imagine the possibilities in growing and going!

Investigative Questions:

1) Which do you feel is more in control of you: your heart, your mind, or your soul? Why? Do you feel that is healthy? Why or why not?

2) Which part do you think you still need to strengthen the most: your heart, your mind, or your soul? Explain.

3) What does "made in God's image" mean to you?

4) Do you see the image of God within you? Why or why not?

5) Do you see the image of God in others? Why or why not?

Action Item:

Ask three friends when they feel the most "whole." At worship? At work? Participating in a hobby? Do they see the coming together of heart, mind, and soul? Why or why not?

Chapter 2
C: Corporate Worship
Who's Who in Worship

What does it mean to worship with the Body of Christ? It means worshiping with people you know *and* with people you don't know, with people you agree with *and* with people you disagree with, with people who are similar to you *and* with people who are vastly different from you. It's all about worshiping with your fellow followers of Jesus, where sometimes the *only* thing you have in common is... Jesus! It means worshiping for the sake of connecting to Jesus within a community of other sinful human beings, and knowing that even though we may be very different from one another, we are still united, still one in Christ. There is something powerful about worshiping with the Body of Christ!

One of the most poignant worship experiences my wife and I have ever been blessed to be a part of was at an international church in Bangkok, Thailand. Every shade and color of people you can imagine were present in God's house that day. The pastor was Canadian. The worship leader was from Australia. The family behind us was from China. The family to the side of us was from Africa. The man in front of us was an American – and he gave me a Thai Bible that God would use to lead someone to Christ ten years later in Southern California! This international worship service was perhaps the closest thing I have seen to a heavenly assembly on this side of eternity.

Although we spoke different languages, and looked, dressed, and acted differently, we were one in Jesus! Our diversity is a blessing, not a curse!

The profound mystery that is the life, death, and resurrection of Jesus connects believers together, even if we appear to have nothing else in common. As St. Paul says in Ephesians 4:3-6:

> Make every effort to keep the unity of the Spirit through the bond of peace. There is one body and one Spirit, just as you were called to one hope when you were called; one Lord, one faith, one baptism; one God and Father of all, who is over all and through all and in all.

What I love most about traveling the world and engaging with other cultures is that in spite of our differences, we are the same in Christ! We are all sinners in need of the forgiveness we receive through Jesus. We need to be reminded often that God loves the whole world, not just me and my family and my friends, and not just the people in my own church. God doesn't just love the people that I love, or those that look and act like me. This is one of those basic truths that might seem quite obvious, but it can still be an awakening when we actually see it in action!

One of the movements in the modern church is to have home churches made up of a few families in the neighborhood, or small organic churches that gather in coffee shops or bars. And while these can be effective, the fear I have for them is they tend to surround us with people who look, think, and act just like we do. It can be difficult for us to be challenged and to grow spiritually if everyone around us is too similar to us. When we limit our view of others, we limit our view of God. And limiting our view of God – of the way He thinks, whom He loves, or what He is capable of doing – is a very dangerous thing. As Job says in Job 11:7, "Can you fathom the mysteries of God? Can you probe the limits of the Almighty?" No, I can't – and neither can you. But together we enter into the mystery, knowing that God is bigger than our wildest imaginations. We are worshiping Him "who is able to do immeasurably more than all we ask or imagine" (Ephesians 3:20). God is beyond our wildest imaginations. The moment we put God into a box, He breaks the box. He's unlimited!

There is something healthy about worshiping with people we don't know or agree with (or even like!) because it reminds us that God is so much bigger than us – bigger than our circle of friends, our ideas, and our own ways of doing things. God is God, and He loves the whole world with a passionate, unending love. When we are worshiping with strangers, we are reminded just how big He is! Worshiping with cultures different than ours will also give us a glimpse of this. Try attending a worship service in a different language sometime – it will remind you of how big God is! Over the years, I have spent a fairly significant amount of time worshiping with friends on the White Mountain Apache Reservation in Arizona. When I worship in the Apache language, I only understand one word that is spoken: *JESUS* – and really, that's the only word that matters!

Martin Luther King, Jr. said that Sunday mornings are the most segregated time in America.[1] Research shows us that the vast majority of Americans have never worshiped in a church where they were the ethnic minority. Could this be contributing to the continued racial divide in our country?

When we limit our view of others, we limit our view of God

We tend to focus great amounts of energy on the *how, where,* and *when* of worship, when the most important question is the *who*. As Neil Cole says, "All along the right question is – *Who*? Where you worship is nothing compared to who it is you worship."[2] The Who is Jesus, the Savior of the world!

I long for an end to the worship wars, where for decades followers of Jesus have been fighting over the "how," "where," and "when" questions about worship. If you love the organ – great! My mother is an organist, so I am a big fan of organs! If you love the praise band – great! I married a praise band worship leader, so I love praise bands! Diversity in worship style and structure is a strength, not a weakness. Different people will connect with different styles. I encourage you to investigate different worship styles. God is speaking through all of them, and it just might be good for you to engage in a worship experience that is out of your comfort zone. It's a great way to be reminded that God is much bigger than your comfort zone! Being a Missionary Disciple is really all about shattering comfort zones!

Investigative Questions:

1) How is your corporate worship life?

2) Is this something that needs to be a higher priority for you? How can corporate worship help you discover identity, mission, and purpose?

3) How can one be "on mission" during corporate worship? How does mission fit in with worship?

Action Item:

Visit a Christian church this weekend that is vastly different than your own – perhaps culturally or ethnically. Or attend a worship service in a different language. Notice the differences – and look for things that you share in common. Make sure to talk and personally connect with a few people while you are there.

Jesus Was No Pew Potato!

Jesus went to church. Have you ever thought about that before? He went to the temple and synagogue regularly, and fulfilled all of the requirements of being a "good Jew." He religiously remembered the Sabbath day and kept it holy. What's more, Jesus didn't just sit passively in the first-century version of a pew – He was an active participant in the worship experience!

This was modeled for Him by His parents. Luke 2:22-24 tells us:

> When the time came for the purification rites required by the Law of Moses, Joseph and Mary took him to Jerusalem to present him to the Lord (as it is written in the Law of the Lord, "Every firstborn male is to be consecrated to the Lord"), and to offer a sacrifice in

keeping with what is said in the Law of the Lord: "a pair of doves or two young pigeons."

Jesus' parents raised Him to take corporate worship and its rites and rituals very seriously – and He did. What a powerful reminder for parents today!

There is also the great story (found in Luke 2:41-52) of Jesus getting "lost" at the temple when He was twelve years old. If you aren't familiar with the story, let me share it with you. Jesus and His family were visiting the temple for the Passover festival – the very same festival during which (about 20 years later) Jesus instituted the Lord's Supper and changed the meaning of the Passover forever. On the way home from the temple, there was a large caravan of family members heading in the same direction. Mary and Joseph realized three days into the trip home that they could not find Jesus anywhere.

So they hurried all the way back to the temple, and sure enough, Jesus was sitting in the temple courts, teaching. When questioned by His worried mother as to why He was still there, Jesus responded, "Didn't you know I had to be in my Father's house?" (v. 49).

Going to church was a priority for Jesus. He knew it was a place of learning and a place of teaching. It was a place of community for Him, and the "house" of His heavenly Father. Do you ever feel that kind of longing in your soul, that strong need from deep down inside, to come to church to worship? We were made that way. We were created to worship! And yet, we sometimes allow our lives to become so busy and so filled with distractions that we get pulled into a hundred other directions, and then going to church isn't a high priority for us.

But it was for Jesus! If the Son of God felt the need to be there frequently with His heavenly Father, then how much more do *we* need it!

So we can see that even from His youth, Jesus was an active participant in the worship experience. He wasn't just a pew potato! Luke chapter 4 gives us an account of Jesus reading and interpreting Scripture as a part of worship. *The IVP New Testament Commentary Series* says:

> To appreciate the account, it helps to understand the order of an ancient synagogue service ... . To have a synagogue service required the presence of ten adult males. At the service, the Shema was recited (Deuteronomy 6:4-9), followed by prayers, including some set prayers like the Tephillah and the Eighteen Benedictions ... . After this the Scripture was read, beginning with a portion from the Torah (Genesis – Deuteronomy) and moving next to a section from the Prophets. Instruction then followed. Often the speaker linked the texts together through appeal to other passages. The service then closed with a benediction.[1]

Jewish worship is very structured. Read the account of Jesus' participation in Luke 4:14-22. It seems that Jesus was reading during the section on the prophets, and then He added some instruction of His own as well. Jesus models for us that corporate worship is not a passive event, but rather a participatory one.

In addition to reading Scripture and following the structure of worship, we also participate through our tithes and offerings. This was also true in Jesus' time, except it wasn't optional. It was a mandatory "tax" – and to be a respected member of the community, one had to pay it. This was a sticking point for the enemies of Jesus, so they asked a clueless Peter, "Doesn't your teacher pay the temple tax?" (Matthew 17:24). Now, Jesus did not make a salary being the Son of God. He was dependent upon others for His basic needs, so to resolve His temple tax issue, He told Peter, "Go to the lake and throw out your line. Take the first fish you catch; open its mouth and you will find a four-drachma coin. Take it and give it to them for my tax and yours" (Matthew 17:27).

Jesus made sure He paid the temple tax, even though He knew of the corruption with the temple hierarchy. He knew it was important to "Give back to Caesar what is Caesar's and to God what is God's" (Mark 12:17). Considering that God is the creator of everything, why shouldn't we joyfully and willingly give back to Him?

The church that I'm currently a member of practices a "children's church" model, where at a specific point in the service the kids are taken to a different room for age-appropriate teaching. When asked what elements of the corporate worship experience I wanted my kids to be present for, I said singing, the sacraments, and the offering. Most people agree with me on the first two, but I get many questions on the last one. Why would you want your kids to observe the offering when they could be somewhere else learning more about Jesus?

Participating in the offering *is* learning about Jesus! We need to teach our kids what the offering is. It's a giving back to God of our first fruits. Giving is a part of our mission. Giving is a discipline. Giving is a gift from God that reminds us that all things belong to Him anyway. Too often in the offering conversation, we focus on amounts and percentages. Don't. Focus on giving generously. Giving is not about equal percentages but equal sacrifice. If you are a starving college student with more student loans than you can count, give generously what you can. If you are a millionaire, give generously what you can. (And if you are a millionaire, I have some great mission project ideas that I would love to talk with you about…)

Perhaps the most famous (or infamous) account of Jesus at the temple happened on the Monday of Holy Week. Jesus was furious at the money changers in the temple and He angrily drove them out. In doing so, He said, "It is written, … 'My house will be called a house of prayer,' but you are making it 'a den of robbers'" (Matthew 21:13). I find it fascinating to watch a ticked-off Jesus! If it angers Jesus that the house of God is misused, then it should also anger us to see such things!

The exact verse Jesus quotes here is Isaiah 56:7 – "For my house will be called a house of prayer for all nations." Notice that yet again we are reminded of the universal message of Jesus. He desires *all* nations to know Him as Lord and Savior – not just ours! Worship is a mission in and of itself! Worship is a place where those who do not know Jesus can connect to Him.

By the way, Jesus is also quoting the Old Testament when He uses the phrase "den of robbers." In Jeremiah 7:11 the prophet says, "Has this house, which bears my Name, become a den of robbers to you? But I have been watching! declares the LORD." There are two things for us to take from this scene in the temple. First, Jesus knows His Scripture well, and so should we! Second, human beings have been cheating people in the name of God for a very, very long time. The house of God, the church building (never forgetting that the church is not a building, but the people!), needs to be a place where people of every tribe and tongue can come together in peace and unity for corporate worship! Nobody should be treated unfairly or dishonestly within its walls.

One can also be "robbed" at church when God's grace is not lived out by church members. Again, I have the opportunity to visit many different churches, and in some churches – as a complete stranger – no one will say a word to me, until I'm introduced as a "church celebrity." Then, interestingly enough, many people will come say "Hi!"

You can be a missionary at church by simply saying "Hi," and showing love, kindness, and compassion to people you don't know. They might be there for the first time – great, get to know them. They might be a founding member that you just haven't met yet – great, get to know them! It might feel uncomfortable at first, but you don't ever want to be the reason someone doesn't come back to church.

People can also be cheated at church when the focus is not on Jesus and His mission. Infighting and politics run rampant in many churches. The sanctuary from the storm can quickly become the eye of the storm. I have visited more than a few churches where I've heard nothing but politics from the pulpit. When stuck in these realities, how can you be a bridge builder? How can you be a part of the solution instead of part of the problem? How can you live in grace, and let others live in grace?

Corporate worship will no doubt help you discover your identity as a Missionary Disciple. To maximize this opportunity, participate! Serve as an usher, greeter, acolyte, reader, instrumentalist, vocalist, tech person, etc. Simply serve. Serving leads to growing, and growing leads to serving. By participating, you will increase focus as well as your learning and growth. And who knows? You just might help someone else feel comfortable in that space – and that's missions!

Investigative Questions:

1) How did (or didn't) your parents model for you the importance of corporate worship?

2) If applicable, how are you modeling it for your kids – or how do you plan to, someday?

3) How are you actively participating in corporate worship? What else could you do?

Chapter 2 – C: Corporate Worship

4) Is giving your tithes and offerings important to you? Why or why not?

5) Do you think your church building is a house of prayer today? Why or why not?

6) Have you ever felt cheated in some way at church? If so, what happened?

Action Item:

Find a new way to participate in the corporate worship experience. Maybe it's in an official capacity, like an usher or greeter. Or maybe it's unofficial – for example, sitting with someone who's alone. Maybe it's by bringing your Bible and following along during the readings. Maybe it's bringing a friend and teaching them what the worship experience is all about. How can you increase your participation in corporate worship? How can you be on mission even during worship?

Ideas for You to Investigate

Finding Your Sanctuary

One of the beautiful things about the church today is the degree of variety and social diversity that can be found. If a traditional service with wooden pews and a pipe organ isn't your style, there are countless other options for you to choose from. Nowadays, you can find a worship service with just about any type or style of music. In some churches in the UK, they are using "worship DJs" who play club-sounding music in the worship experience. Here in Texas, we have "cowboy churches" held in barns where you not only may bring your gun (no joke, it's legal!) but you can also listen to country-western-style worship music!

Some churches are very traditional and liturgical, while others are very informal. Some have the congregation chant, respond, and recite, while others have preachers/teachers who are looking for interaction and discussion during the teaching time. In some churches you will feel out of place if you are not wearing a tie, while in others, like the church I served in

Hawaii, only first-time visitors wore ties... and usually by the third visit, they wouldn't even be wearing shoes!

As you think about finding a church, think paradox: Find something that feels comfortable to you, but also challenges and stretches you. Live in the tension, you Missionary Disciple!

The church is a hospital for sinners. It's a place for imperfect people. It's a sanctuary from the storm.

I love to ask church-work students, "Do you want to attend a church where you agree with everything that is said from the pulpit?" Many don't know how to answer the question, so I often give my opinion before they reply: *No!* I want corporate worship to be uplifting and unifying, but also challenging and thought-provoking. I want the worship experience to be the pep talk given in the locker room before the big game. Too often we think that the church service is the game – but *life* is the game. The corporate worship experience encourages us and prepares us for the game, and keeps us focused and centered on what is important. I want a worship service that puts thought and effort into the worship expressions, where excellence is modeled in all aspects. I care much less about style, and much more about quality. Whatever you are looking for, make sure that you find something that works for you and stretches you!

Sometimes people will say to me, "I haven't been to church in a long time. I've tried several, but I just haven't found one I like." If you can't find a congregation you feel comfortable with, I encourage you to think about a few things. First, is what you are looking for realistic? There is no perfect church. Every church is made up of sinners in need of God's grace. There is no perfect worship experience this side of heaven.

Second, instead of looking for something outside of yourself to satisfy your needs, perhaps you should look at whether there's something inside of you that's in need of change. It's akin to the relationship advice, "Don't look for Mr. Right – work on being Ms. Right."

Does your dissatisfaction stem from the churches you have visited, or is the problem something that's unsettled inside of you? Maybe you (or someone close to you) had an unpleasant or even hurtful experience with a congregation in the past, and now you are hesitant to get involved again with a church. Or maybe you have some doubts about your faith and aren't sure exactly what you believe – so you don't feel comfortable coming to church because you think that you need to have everything "figured out" spiritually before you can attend.

The church is a hospital for sinners. It's a place for imperfect people. It's a sanctuary from the storm. So, if you are an imperfect sinner with a stormy life – it's the place for you! Kara Powell, in her book *Growing Young*, talks about how doubt can be a good thing.[1] To clarify, doubt can be good if – and only if – it is explored and expressed. Silence is toxic, not doubt. That is what church should be: a place to ask your questions, wrestle with answers, engage with like- and different-minded people, receive God's grace, learn and grow. If you are perfect and have life all figured out, then corporate worship is not the place for you.

One of my recent graduates started working with a parachurch organization. During a meeting where she was telling me about her mission and ministry, I threw her what I thought was a softball question that I ask all employees of parachurch ministries: "What do you do when someone comes to faith in Jesus through your ministry?"

She was speechless at first, and finally said that she had no idea. I felt like such a failure as a teacher! How could she have taken so many of my classes, and not know the answer to that all-important question?! When someone comes to faith in Jesus, the next natural step is to connect them to a Christian community, a.k.a., a church! Corporate worship is a perfect place to start, so connect them to a believing community right away.

Investigative Questions:

1) What are you looking for in a corporate worship experience? Why?

2) If you grew up attending a church, do you want to find one that is similar to what you grew up with? Or would you prefer something different? Explain.

3) If you have been hurt by a bad experience while attending a church, I am so sorry! I encourage you to process the hurt with someone, and "name" it. Churches don't hurt people – people hurt people. How can you, by God's grace, work through your hurt? As God redeems your hurt, do not be surprised when He uses your story and experiences to help someone else!

4) What adjectives would you use to describe your ideal worship experience?

Action Item:

Attend a worship service in a different style than you are used to or prefer. Learn why they worship in that way. Learn about the history of that style. Find someone who appears to really enjoy that style, and ask them what makes that style so meaningful for them. Can you articulate why you prefer to worship the way that you usually do?

Come and See!

Maybe the best way to think about what kind of church you are looking for is to ask yourself, *Would I invite my friends to come experience this with me?* When you see an enjoyable or thought-provoking movie or show, or find a new binge-worthy series on Netflix, one of the first things you want to do is tell other people about it. When you hear a great new song or discover a band that you are excited about, you can't keep it to yourself. When a cause moves you to be compassionate, be it human trafficking or poverty, you are compelled to do something and get others involved as well.

What if our worship experience was the same way? What if we were so excited and passionate about worship that we simply had to invite others to participate? St. Paul tells us in Romans 1:16, "For I am not ashamed of the Gospel, because it is the power of God that brings salvation to everyone who believes." I truly believe that the majority of Christians are not ashamed of the Gospel. We know that the Gospel is the power of God working through the person of Jesus for the salvation of all who believe. So why don't more of us invite our unchurched friends to church like they're giving away hundred-dollar bills? If we're not ashamed of the Gospel, then perhaps we are embarrassed by our church and our worship style. Are we concerned that our unchurched friends will find our worship boring and not relevant to real life? Are we boring people to death with the Gospel – or at least how we are presenting it?

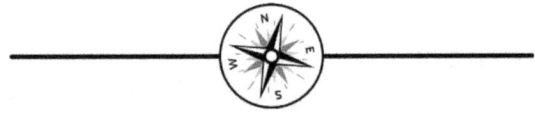

The best witnessing method is not billboards, newspaper ads, or television commercials – it's a personal invitation from a believer to an unbeliever

The movie *The Greatest Showman* is not an accurate history lesson on the life and times of P.T. Barnum, but it is certainly a fun musical. On the DVD extras, the star Hugh Jackman tells the story of attempting to get the movie financed. Hugh was scheduled to sing the songs and do a basic read-through of the script for a group of financers. Unfortunately, he got skin cancer and had to have the malignancy removed. He received 70 stitches on the inside of his nose, with these instructions from his doctor: *Do not sing.* During the presentation, Hugh is doing a good job not singing until he reaches the film's climactic song where his character realizes the error of his ways and now gets to make amends. Hugh Jackman cannot help himself. He sings his heart out! And his singing becomes contagious! The rest of the choir and performers sing brighter and bolder because their leader is putting everything he has into his performance. In the video you can see him touching his nose periodically to make sure he's not bleeding – but he's so moved by the moment that he *has* to sing! Worship should move us like that!

Almost everyone agrees that the best witnessing method is not billboards, newspaper ads, or television commercials – it's a personal invitation from a believer to an unbeliever. If we want our people to bring their unchurched friends to a worship service, we need to create an environment that they are not embarrassed to invite others to visit. We cannot have churches that are stuffy and uninviting, if we want the unchurched to walk through the doors. By God's grace and the power of the Holy Spirit, we need to do anything and everything to create an environment that people are excited to share.

Dr. Andrew Walls, in his book *The Cross-Cultural Process in Christian History,* reminds us that in the history of Christianity there has never been a convert in a vacuum.[1] Converts have always come in the context of community. We need to be inviting people who do not know Jesus to church.

Even if we attend a vibrant church that we love, we might still be hesitant to invite others. Maybe we don't feel as if we have the right words to ask a friend to come with us to church. But it could be as simple as borrowing the words of Philip. In the first chapter of John's Gospel, we see that Philip really wanted his good friend Nathaniel to meet Jesus. Nathaniel, however, was not interested in this invitation, and just made fun of Jesus' hometown: "Nazareth! Can anything good come from there?" But Philip's response to him is so simple and beautiful: "Come and see" (John 1:46). Nathaniel *did* come and see – and sure enough, he became a dedicated follower and one of the twelve original disciples! If you are not sure what to say to invite someone, try these words: "Come and see." Missionary Disciples trust that Jesus will take it from there!

Investigative Questions:

1) Who could you invite to church with you? What caused you to think of these people?

2) What factors might be preventing you from inviting your friends to church?

3) How can you help create an environment at your church that people will not be embarrassed by?

4) If your friends agree to "come and see" your church, what will they see?

Action Item:

Invite someone to come to church with you this weekend! If they say no, don't take it personally. Trust that God is at work, and think of other ways to invite or connect them to Jesus.

The Sacred Experienced

I have a complete love of the sacraments. They are experiential. They are God's way of giving us a physical touch. They are beautiful and tangible images of the forgiveness and salvation that God promises to His people. The sacraments are commanded by Jesus, and are where heaven and earth collide through the eternal Word of God and the earthly elements of water, bread, and wine.

Martin Luther was fond of saying "I *am* baptized," rather than "I *was* baptized."[1] Baptism is a combination of past, present, future – eternity. It's an entering into God's family forever. Baptism is a washing and cleansing that was even foreshadowed in the Old Testament through the story of Noah's ark: God used water to cleanse sin from the world.

The churches that I grew up in practiced sprinkling water on babies, children, and adults during the rite of baptism. And that is beautiful. But I also want to tell you about a church I visited in the middle of nowhere in Alaska – a town called Galena. It was a Baptist church and it needed a baptistery that was large enough to hold an adult person, but small enough to be kept warm on the coldest Alaskan winter day. So they ended up buying a coffin and turning it into their baptismal font. What a beautiful reminder that through baptism, we are given new life! We are dead in our sins but because of Jesus' resurrection, we are resurrected too!

At the same time, baptism is about the Word of God – not about the water. I had the privilege of baptizing my nephew at a church in Las Vegas, Nevada. We reviewed the promises of baptism, asked all the right questions, prayed together, and then headed over to the baptismal font to baptize the baby and… there was no water in the font! When I later recounted this story to a group of preschoolers during chapel time, I asked them, "What should I have done?"

A little hand went in the air. I called on the child, who immediately yelled out, "Spit!" And he's right – spit would provide enough water for a legitimate baptism! (Just to let you know how the story really ended: Some of the ladies in the church provided us with a nice bowl of warm water from a nearby sink, and everything worked out fine! But that spitting idea is a creative one…)

I was baptized when I was five days old. I do not remember it at all – but God does! I am an advocate of baptizing babies. It's a beautiful connection to the Old Testament covenant of circumcision. Baptism is an outward sign of an inward faith. I like to think that baptizing babies is a little like Opening Day in Major League Baseball. In other sports, the most important day of the season is the final game, like the Super Bowl. But in baseball, where it's been said that hope springs eternal, Opening Day is the most important day because everyone is in first place. No matter how bad your team was last year, this could be their year! They all start off in first place, not because of anything they have done but because of who they are: a major league baseball team. Of all sports, baseball has the longest season, with 162 games per year. It's a grind, full of ups and downs, strikeouts and home runs. The greatest players in the game fail seven out of ten times at bat! But to the faithful, there is the promise of the post-season – the season *after* the season. This is the time when champions are crowned. But to get there, it all starts with Opening Day!

Our baptism is the start of our new life in Jesus! Following Jesus means that we will have many ups and downs in our life. We will strike out, and we will hit some home runs. But the promise is that all who believe can say with St. Paul, "I have finished the race, I have kept the faith" (2 Timothy 4:7)! Remember the goal of baseball is to get "home." For followers of Jesus – heaven is our home!²

The Lord's Supper is the ultimate foretaste of the feast to come. We partake of Jesus' true body and blood through the earthly elements of bread and wine. We get a taste of forgiveness and salvation. There are three common names for the sacrament of the altar: The Lord's Supper, Communion, and Eucharist. All three of these names give us insight into what's happening during the sacrament. "The Lord's Supper" shows the family dinner aspect of the ritual, and connects directly to the Jewish Seder meal (more on the Seder in a couple paragraphs). "Communion" shows the unity of the Body of Christ as we celebrate Christ's life, death, and resurrection together. And the word "Eucharist" literally means "thanksgiving." The sacrament is done in thanksgiving for what God did in and through Jesus.

Different churches offer the Lord's Supper at different times – some twice a month, others every week, etc. I get asked all the time how often one should take it. And my answer is, "As often as you can!" At the last church where I served, we had five services, which meant I got to take the supper five times per week. Once a student asked me if I really needed to take it five times and I said, "Of course – I sinned since I'd taken it last time!"

If you've never experienced a Jewish Seder meal, make sure to attend one this Lenten season! You will see how Jesus took the story of the Exodus and the ritual of the Seder meal and redeemed it step by step! In the Seder there are actually four glasses of wine per person, but each one has special significance and meaning. The third cup is called the cup of redemption, and many theologians believe it is during this cup that Jesus instituted the Lord's Supper. Communion is a meal that is two thousand years old, brought out of a meal that is four thousand years old – all to grow eternity in our hearts today.[3]

The sacraments were designed by God to connect the ancient with the future. The sacraments allow us to feel, touch, taste, and experience the promises of God in a community. As you find a corporate worship experience, examine their use of the sacraments, and be sure to participate regularly.

Investigative Questions:

1) What does your baptism mean to you?

2) How do you see baptism connecting to the story of Noah's ark and the flood (Genesis 6-9)?

3) What is your favorite name for the sacrament of the altar: The Lord's Supper, Communion, or Eucharist? Why do you prefer it?

4) What does partaking of the Lord's Supper mean to you? Why do you feel that it's important?

5) How do you see Communion connecting to the Passover and Seder meal?

Action Item:

What if this year, in addition to celebrating your birthday, you celebrated your baptismal birthday? Do you know when and how you were baptized? How could you find out? Ask someone who was at your baptism to tell you what they remember about that day.

Don't Just Sit There...

"The Son of Man did not come to be served, but to serve" (Matthew 20:28). Following Jesus means a life of serving. A Missionary Disciple is a servant. Perhaps the best way to connect the dots on the tension between discipleship and missions is to serve at the place you call your church home.

When my family moved to Texas in 2009, and I started serving at Concordia University, we were able to "pick" a church home for the first time in our marriage. (Previously, we had attended whichever congregation I had been called to.) We told ourselves that we were going to church-shop for six months, and just sit in the pews to be "fed." That lasted two whole weeks, because after visiting the first church, I was quickly preaching and Christy was in the band. Missionary Disciples serve.

I love serving at church with my family. My wife is a gifted worship leader; I do a fair amount of preaching and speaking; and lately we have been able to get our daughters plugged in by singing with the band, reading Scripture, and serving in the nursery. I've been blessed to team-teach with all of them. We've volunteered in children's ministry together. It is so much fun for us to all serve together as a family!

Once you have found a place, a corporate worshiping body, how will you serve? Remember that the church is not the building – it is the *people*! And many different people are needed to make the worship experience happen. Maybe you can volunteer with the children's or youth ministries. Or maybe you can join a musical ensemble or choir – or if you're a techie, those groups always need sound people! Perhaps you can help usher or take the offering, or distribute bulletins or handouts. Maybe you can read the Scripture lessons aloud during the service. You could be a friendly greeter at the door, welcoming people as they come in. Or you can help answer questions and guide first-time visitors who are looking for the nursery or Sunday School. Helping people who look confused may be the most important way to serve! Whatever your skill level or experience, there is a way you can serve!

When my kids were young, their favorite way to serve the church was to stand up in front with a wicker basket during Communion, and as people walked by, they placed their little Communion cups into the basket that one of the girls was holding. It is quite possibly the simplest job ever invented. A chair could do the job just fine. But, my kids *loved* serving in this way. They fought over it! They bragged about it to their friends!

There are also things that need to be done behind the scenes. Do you love cuddling babies and playing with little children? Then consider helping out in the church nursery, so that parents of young children can have a precious hour of uninterrupted time to worship and connect with God. What a wonderful gift you will be providing to those who need it!

Each of us can serve in some way. How are *you* going to serve? I can tell you firsthand that it is a ministry leader's dream to have someone walk up to them and ask, "How can I serve?" You may have to get the smelling salts ready, because they might pass out due to excitement and shock! There is no better way to gain "ownership" of and connectivity to a church than to serve. You will also get to know more people in your congregation, and form deeper relationships with them, by serving together. And if you ever find yourself tempted to skip church on Sunday mornings, then just knowing that others are counting on your participation (and looking forward to seeing you!) will help you fight the urge to stay in bed!

Asking your unchurched friends to serve with you could be a great introduction to your church. It gives them a reason and purpose for being there. While certainly different churches have different guidelines as to which roles non-members can serve in, I have seen people come to faith in Jesus through serving in ways like the praise band or nursery. Service opportunities can be ways for people to hear the Gospel for the very first time!

There is a church I have visited in New York City that has developed a relationship with the Jewish synagogue next door. During the high holy days, the church and the synagogue help each other out by sending over their ushers and elders as volunteers. This means the ushers and elders of the Jewish synagogue are hearing the Gospel on Christmas and Easter! Providing service opportunities may not feel like mission work, but any opportunity for people to hear the Gospel is absolutely mission work!

Investigative Questions:

1) How have you served in a corporate worship experience in the past? What did it mean to you? Have you had any negative experiences while serving?

2) Do you have any fears about serving? If so, what are they? What are some ways you can move past those fears?

3) What are some of your talents and gifts, and how could you use them in your current (or future) corporate worship setting?

Action Item:

You do not need an official title to serve. You might be able to serve best in a way that has not been offered or revealed yet. Imagine different and unique ways to serve – maybe in ways that no one has ever served before! Attempt to invent a new way to serve! I encourage you to talk with your pastor and other leaders about how your ideas can be implemented in your church.

Chapter 3
S: Small Group

Good Things Come in Small Packages

While corporate worship tends to be large and not very intimate, small groups are the exact opposite form of community. I define a small group as a group of two to twelve people who gather to know and be known by each other for the purpose of spiritual growth, accountability, support, and common mission. Whether you call it small group, support group, life group, prayer partners, or accountability partners, the main objectives are the same. We need to have the outside perspective of others in order to better understand ourselves. We always view ourselves differently than others do.

Do you remember the first time you heard a recording of your voice? I bet you thought, *Wow, really? I sound like that?* My wife has an absolutely beautiful voice. However, she hates listening to her own voice recordings. It's a rather amusing way to tease her – I just have her listen to the voicemails she leaves me. She hates it! She always asks me, "Do I really sound like that?!"

We can have blinders on when it comes to who we are, especially in our attitudes and behaviors. The outside perspective that others can offer us helps uncover those areas where we might need to grow or make some changes.

When I grade my students' presentations, I have a space on my grading rubric for "vocal idiosyncrasies," meaning: *um, ahhh, like, you know*, etc. When a student has one, I will always ask them if they know what it is – and they usually do not. But once it is pointed out, I've been told that they then hear my voice every time they catch themselves saying it! I think this is a compliment...?

Think about the power that comes from taking those blinders off and being honest. The late great baseball player, Tony Gwynn, was one of the first major league baseball players who used game film to improve his hitting. He would spend hours and hours watching himself on video, making corrections, and seeking wisdom from coaches and trusted friends. The results pretty much speak for themselves: Tony was a First Ballot Hall of Famer, and one of the greatest hitters of a generation – all because he was willing to take the blinders off and examine his actions and habits through the lenses of many other people.

It is not good for people to live in isolation. There is great value in intimate community. In the creation account of Genesis 1-2, early on God says everything is "good"! All the days of creation are "good," and the creation of Man is even "very good." But then seemingly out of the blue, God says, *Not good!* What's not good? "It is not good for the man to be alone. I will make a helper suitable for him" (Genesis 2:18). Loneliness is not good. God then created a suitable helper – more people! The animals were not adequate companions. We need to be around other people!

We were created for community, and that community needs to be a safe place and a sanctuary. While the origin of the word sanctuary means "sacred place," it is powerful to realize that our modern understanding of a sanctuary is a place of safety and refuge. There is great safety in the sacred. Our understanding of "small group" needs to be both safe and sacred.

I love the song "Sanctuary." The chorus is:

> *Lord, prepare me to be a sanctuary*
> *Pure and holy, tried and true*
> *With thanksgiving, I'll be a living*
> *Sanctuary for You*[1]

Do you realize what you're praying when you sing this song? You're asking God to make *you* a sacred and safe place. You're asking God to dwell inside of you, so that you can be a sacred and safe place for others. It isn't about you – it's about being a blessing for other people. We thank God that we are blessed to be a blessing to others!

Our world is becoming more and more crowded. There are over seven and a half billion people on the planet.[2] Just look at that number: 7,500,000,000. Can you image what that number would look like on a check with your name on it? It's huge! Interestingly enough, people can still feel very alone in a crowded place. Without personal connections, the crowd merely becomes a sea of faces or ideas, not individuals. It's so easy to feel lost, small, and insignificant. But in a small group, no one needs to feel alone. People often feel more comfortable speaking and sharing within the intimacy of a small group. Large groups can be intimidating, especially for those who tend to be more quiet and shy. There is intimacy in the safe and sacred place.

A small group not only provides community, but it also expands our insight into prayer, Scripture, worship, morals, values, and the other spiritual disciplines. Studying with others strengthens everyone. We are better together. As King Solomon says in Ecclesiastes 4:12, "Though one may be overpowered, two can defend themselves. A cord of three strands is not quickly broken." There is great power in numbers!

Think about the guiding principles of a small group. While every group will be different, there should be some non-negotiables. Some groups even have covenants – or promises – that they make to each other. For example: *We will keep things shared confidential. We will praise in public and critique in private. If there are disagreements, we will resolve peacefully or agree to disagree peacefully. We will let other group members know when we cannot attend.*

If you join a small group and it doesn't seem to work for you, then I encourage you to keep looking to find another group that is a better fit for you. Don't give up on small groups if you aren't happy with the first one you try. Not every group will appeal to every individual due to various personalities, backgrounds, etc. I promise you there are many groups out there that are right for you! And if you can't easily find a small group that fits you, consider starting your own, and invite others to join you! At least, that's what a Missionary Disciple would do.

Investigative Questions:

1) How is your small group life? Is this something that needs to be a higher priority for you?

2) How can a small group help you discover who you are?

3) What covenant items would you desire in a small group?

4) How can you locate a small group?

Action Item:

Join a small group. Commit to one month at first. Start slowly and watch God work!

The Ultimate Small-Group Leader

Is it OK to have favorite students? A common critique I hear about professors and youth ministers (as those are the two main circles I run in) is that they sometimes pick favorites. I have always looked down upon this practice – I try never to show favoritism, and I try to love all of my students equally. Interestingly enough, someone pointed out to me recently that Jesus "picked favorites," at least when it came to who He would train to be His first disciples! I guess I had never thought about it that way before. He picked twelve disciples to be in his small group. Mark 3:13-19:

> Jesus went up on a mountainside and called to him those he wanted, and they came to him. He appointed twelve that they might be with him and that he might send them out to preach and to have authority to drive out demons. These are the twelve he appointed: Simon (to whom he gave the name Peter), James son of Zebedee and his brother John (to them he gave the name Boanerges, which means "sons of thunder"),

Andrew, Philip, Bartholomew, Matthew, Thomas, James son of Alphaeus, Thaddaeus, Simon the Zealot and Judas Iscariot, who betrayed him.

Now certainly we can tie the number twelve back to the Old Testament and the twelve tribes of Israel, named after the twelve sons of the patriarch Jacob, son of Isaac, and grandson of Abraham. The number twelve is a connecting point for the old and new covenants. And the Scriptures are clear as to *what* He called them to do: preach, heal, and drive out demons (Mark 6:12-13). They came from a variety of backgrounds; there was a tax collector, a few fishermen, some "zealots," and maybe even a few unemployed people! They were definitely not all well-respected people and pillars of their community! So why did Jesus pick *these* twelve? Only God knows! If we look at this question personally, why did God choose *me*? Why did God choose *you*? He calls us according to His purposes. And thankfully for us, He uses sinners, not perfect people!

In addition to choosing these twelve disciples, Jesus also had an even smaller, closer core group of three others: Peter, James, and John. Why would He need this more intimate subgroup? This again ties back to the Old Testament. In Exodus 24 we see that Moses had his intimate circle of three others, made up of his brother Aaron and his nephews, Nadab and Abihu. Every leader needs an intimate group of trusted advisors who are willing to lend support and encouragement, and, at times, even tell them what they don't want to hear. As our groups grow smaller, they also become stronger, and our relationships within them deepen.

We might wonder what was so special about this trio – Peter, James, and John. This is just speculation, but James and John may be viewed as apostolic "bookends," as church tradition tells us that James was the first of the apostles to be martyred, and John was the last – who in old age was banished to the island of Patmos and wrote the book of Revelation. And Jesus says to Peter:

> Blessed are you, Simon son of Jonah, for this was not revealed to you by flesh and blood, but by my Father in heaven. And I tell you that you are Peter, and on this rock I will build my church, and the gates of Hades will not overcome it. I will give you the keys of the kingdom of heaven; whatever you bind on earth will be bound in heaven, and whatever you loose on earth will be loosed in heaven. (Matthew 16:17-19)

As you can see, Jesus' small groups weren't about picking favorites as much as modeling the value of intimate community. Even Jesus needed to be in a small group, and then an even smaller group. The small groups of Jesus involved deeper teaching. As Mark noted, "He did not say anything to them [the crowds] without using a parable. But when he was alone with his own disciples, he explained everything" (Mark 4:34). Explanation is a crucial part of being in a small group. Jesus was training them to become leaders – and to do so, He had to open up their minds and teach! "He [Jesus] opened their minds so they could understand the Scriptures" (Luke 24:45). Greater understanding of the Scriptures happens in small groups. Questions can be openly asked and answered. Debate and discussion occur. Doubt is explored and expressed. All of this leads to a deeper learning experience.

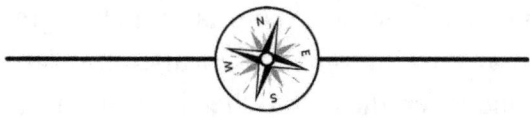

Small groups aren't just about what we can receive from other people, but also about what we can give to others

In Jesus' small groups, we also see accountability. During the Last Supper, He tells His disciples, "Truly I tell you, one of you will betray me" (Matthew 26:21). And when Judas the betrayer responds with, "Surely you don't mean me, Rabbi?" Jesus tells him the difficult truth: "You have said so" (Matthew 26:25). At that very same meal, as Jesus is explaining that He must suffer and die, Peter boasts, "Lord, I am ready to go with you to prison and to death" (Luke 22:33). Boldness on Peter's behalf! This is why many of us love Peter! But Jesus knows his weaknesses, and warns him that "before the rooster crows today, you will deny three times that you know me" (Luke 22:34).

Notice, too, what Jesus says to Peter: "I have prayed for you, Simon, that your faith may not fail. And when you have turned back, strengthen your brothers" (Luke 22:32). This is an important point for us. In small groups, we pray for each other's weaknesses, and we can encourage and strengthen one another through our struggles. In a small group, we openly and honestly acknowledge that life is difficult, but we also realize that it's easier when we walk through it together.

In Jesus' small groups, there is intimacy, grace, forgiveness, and common mission! Even after his denial, Peter is reinstated and given the call to "feed my sheep" (John 21:15-17). Small groups give us opportunities to strengthen others (and be strengthened ourselves) in God's grace and love. When we fall, or when we fail, our group will lift us back on our feet again and help us keep going. Hebrews 10:24-25 says, "And let us consider how we may spur one another on toward love and good deeds, not giving up meeting together, as some are in the habit of doing, but encouraging one another – and all the more as you see the Day approaching." Think about it – there are many who desperately need strength and encouragement. You can be the one, with the help of the Holy Spirit, to lift them up and make a difference in someone's life.

Jesus' small groups were about service to the world. They were the first Missionary Disciples! As they traveled, they not only taught, they also served – they met people's basic needs of food, and physical and spiritual healing. Their intimacy led to greater service. Small groups aren't just about what we can receive from other people, but also about what we can give to others. We need each other!

We can also cling to the promise of Matthew 28:20 that Jesus will be with us always – which means that Jesus is present in our small groups as well. Every group that has followers of Jesus is one of Jesus' small groups.

Investigative Questions:

1) What do you think are the main purposes of a small group? Why are these things important?

2) How do you think Jesus chose His original small group? Do you think you would have chosen different people – perhaps people who were better respected in the community?

3) How does Jesus' example of choosing His small groups help you as you look to join or form a small group?

4) How do you feel about being accountable to others in a group? Does it excite or frighten you? Why?

5) Do you think that holding others accountable is beneficial to them?

Action Item:

Form a small group. Think of three other people – like Jesus' smallest group. Pray about who you will choose and what your common mission will be. Then share your vision and ideas with them, and let them do the same.

Ideas for You to Investigate

Gather Around the Word!

The foundation of any small group needs to be the Word of God. Sure, there is great value in a community having fun together. There is great value in sharing our lives together. There is great value in lifting each other up in prayer. But, the foundation of who we are as believers in Jesus is the Scriptures. One of my concerns with much of Christian education today is that we have turned the Bible into an academic textbook, while it is really meant to be a guidebook for living. It is the book that reveals Jesus to us, and points us to life abundant as well as to life eternal.

As you are looking for a small group (or perhaps forming one), consider what role Scripture plays in the group. The group might be more inclined to work through specific books of the Bible, or maybe they view topical studies to be the best way to explore God's Word. Perhaps another piece of literature or a movie or pop culture element is used in the study. Whichever the case, Scripture needs to be the foundation. I have attended many "Bible" studies where the Bible wasn't even touched! For it to be a true Bible study, the Bible needs to be opened (or turned on, if it's an electronic version!), examined, and explored.

It can be as simple as reading through a specific book of the Bible together. Or maybe your group would be blessed by digging deeper into the weekly text or themes that were preached about on Sunday. Find some good commentaries – there are free ones available online.[1] I also recommend that you get a good study Bible, such as the *Concordia Self-Study Bible*, which features detailed notes at the bottom of each page. The *Serendipity Bible: For Personal and Small Group Study* is another good choice, as it contains life application questions within each chapter. As you read the Word, be looking for life application. How can you apply what you just read to your everyday life and your own personal circumstances? Can you find words of strength and comfort that could be used to help encourage others?

Scripture can basically be divided into two categories: descriptive and prescriptive. Descriptive describes a specific place at a specific time. While learnings can certainly be gleaned from it, it's not a specific command to "go and do likewise." Prescriptive text, on the other hand, is a "prescription" from the Great Physician on how to live life. Both of these can be explored in truth and depth by a small group of believers as they live life together, viewing life through a biblical worldview.

Small groups provide the closeness and intimacy to open up and share our thoughts, insights, and personal experiences in a safe, accepting environment. We can ask questions about the Bible without feeling dumb or ignorant. We can share feelings and doubts about our faith without being judged or misunderstood. Small groups provide the closeness to examine God's Word in depth, and to help one another apply it to our lives.

Life application allows small groups to have a common mission. Too often, small groups are taught that they have to become larger. That may not be the mission of your small group – and that's okay. What will your common mission be? As a group, how will you live out The Great Commandment to fulfill The Great Commission? Are you ready to jump in and explore all that a small group has to offer?

Investigative Questions:

1) Imagine that it is your turn to choose a book of the Bible to study in a small group. Which one would you choose? Why?

2) Thinking back on the small groups you have been a part of, what was the role of the Bible in these groups?

3) What is an example of a part of Scripture that is descriptive? How will you apply this to your life?

4) What is an example of a part of Scripture that is prescriptive? How will you apply this to your life?

Action Item:

Find a book of the Bible you would like to study. Research it and share with others what you have learned and discovered. Invite others to study with you… and, who knows, you just might start a new small group!

Serving Side by Side

If you desire to be missional – to live life as a mission trip – I suggest that you join or form a missional group. This group focuses on the mission of God in the world. This group studies culture and seeks ways to connect the Gospel to culture. To connect, this group constantly and consistently asks three questions:

1) How do we see God the Father at work?
2) What do we see Jesus redeeming and recreating?
3) Where is the Spirit moving us to serve?

These three questions get at the heart of our Trinitarian God: The Father, who created the world and is still actively involved in the world; the Son, who redeemed the world and unconditionally loves the individual (but loves us too much to keep us the way we are); and the Holy Spirit, the power of God who works in and through the heart of humankind and is always at work. The Spirit always desires us to join Him in His work!

If done in a safe and motivated group, these questions can drive and focus our mission to a whole new level! Too often we worry about how we "bring" Jesus to people. Can a human being really "bring" Jesus anywhere? He's omnipresent. He's already there! He's already busy at work redeeming the world – and would love us to join Him.

All of mission falls somewhere on the spectrum from demonstration to declaration. While there needs to be a harmonization of both, usually we are more comfortable with one or the other. Simply put, some of us are much more comfortable demonstrating the Gospel through acts of service, while others prefer the Gospel shared through conversation and dialog. If we only demonstrate, it can be just social work; and if we only declare, it can be just empty words without a foundational relationship and earning the right to be heard. Missional groups live in this tension, seeking to demonstrate *and* declare, and learn their unique context discerning when (and how) either side should be emphasized.

Missional groups personify the Missionary Disciple idea. The group grows together to be of service to the world together. These groups adopt mission projects. Perhaps using Jerusalem, Judea, Samaria, and the Ends of the Earth as a model (see Chapter 5 for more on this, as well as my previous books, *Missional U*[1] and *Missional Too*[2]), these groups dig into God's Word and God's world. These groups may have less structure and format – but their direction will move and flow with the needs of the community and the world.

Depending upon the particular mission, this might be the best group to invite non-Christians to attend. There is something about serving that opens up the heart for receiving the Gospel. Traditionally we have understood that "right teaching" (orthodoxy) leads to "right living" (orthopraxy). But what if the opposite was also true? What if by serving the least fortunate, the servant experiences Jesus at work in them as well? Teaching a concept is the best way to retain it. When one serves in Jesus' name, Jesus works in and through all parties!

Too often we worry about how we "bring" Jesus to people. Can a human being really "bring" Jesus anywhere? He's already there!

My doctoral mentor, Leonard Sweet, likes to refer to the followers of Jesus as "pneumanauts." It's a play on the word astronaut, which is a nautical or sailing term. Astronaut literally means "a sailor of the stars." *Pneuma* (πνεῦμα) is the Greek word for Spirit, so a pneumanaut is a sailor of the Spirit. Wherever the Spirit blows, that is where *we* go! Astronauts may boldly go where no man has gone before, but pneumanauts go where the Spirit is leading – and where Jesus already is!

Investigative Questions:

1) How do you see God the Father at work?

2) What do you see Jesus redeeming and recreating?

3) Where is the Spirit moving you to serve?

Action Item:

Ask a friend – who you think might be up for a new mission – the three questions above. If you find a common mission, you just might have started a missional group!

Stronger Together

Accountability groups can be a powerful tool to overcome a specific sin or issue. Perhaps Alcoholics Anonymous (AA) is the best-known example of this. At every AA meeting, there is a time when participants share their triumphs and struggles. The moment you enter the group, you are given a sponsor who has been where you are and knows how hard it is to get out. This individual is willing to selflessly walk alongside you. In AA, life is not approached from a legalistic perspective but from a position of love, grace, and a desire to grow. This methodology has worked so well that there are now "Anonymous" groups for everything from sex addiction to workaholism to clutter to debt. An up-to-date list on the various anonymous groups can be found online.[1]

Pastor Jonathan Dodson calls his accountability groups "Fight Clubs." If you have ever seen *Fight Club*, the 1999 movie starring Brad Pitt, you know that every fight club needs to have a basic set of rules. For Pastor Dodson, here are his basic Fight Club rules:[2]

1) Know your sin
2) Fight your sin
3) Trust your Savior

Trusting Jesus is vital, in or out of an accountability group. We acknowledge that we are sinful, but we also know that there is nothing we can do about our sin on our own. Jesus overcame our sin on the cross and daily helps us fight our sin.

Accountability groups surround us with others who fight alongside us.

A while back, I had a college student come to me and confess his reliance on pornography. Knowing the statistics that the vast majority of young adult males have experimented with some type of pornography, I asked him if he had ever thought about starting a group of guys who could encourage, love, and support each other through this struggle. At first, he couldn't think of anyone else who was struggling with this specific issue, but after a few weeks, he had gathered a group of about a half dozen young men who entered into a support group together that they called "AccountaBros." They take turns sending daily texts of encouragement and Scripture. They meet once a week as a group to process their week, acknowledge their struggles, and support each other. What a great source of encouragement! The odds of reaching your personal goals increases by 95% when you have an accountability group.[3]

Even if your friend isn't a Christian yet, they can still benefit from accountability! When they see that Christians are normal people who struggle – but know they are forgiven – it could open the door for further Gospel conversations. Accountability could be the tool God uses to bring them into the kingdom!

Accountability is a discipline. Accountability is also part of the discipleship process. Accountability does not have to be a group context. Maybe you need an accountability partner – just one other person. Jesus reminds us in Matthew 18 that when there are two of us gathered in His name, He is there as well! We need each other, and the support we receive and give to others through a trusted accountability group or partner is a huge blessing![4]

Investigative Questions:

1) In what ways would an accountability group or partner be a blessing to you?

2) Is there a specific sin that you could use some help and support fighting? (If you feel comfortable sharing this, what is it?)

3) What would it mean for you to trust your Savior in fighting this sin? Be specific.

4) Can you think of a few people who could be your accountability partners?

Action Item:

Start with one: Ask one person if they would be your accountability partner. Discuss how you will support one another, and what methods you will use (texts, in-person meetings, etc.) The more specific the plan, the easier (and more likely) it is to be carried out.

Partners in Prayer

What do prayer partners do together? Well, the simple answer is that they pray with one another. But it's much more than that! Prayer partners do life together. They pray for each other when they are together and when they are apart. They bounce ideas off of each other, and they hold one another accountable. Prayer partners are in the Word together. They share freely and openly. They know each other very well – the good, the bad, and the ugly! Most importantly, they trust one another and feel safe sharing things.

My prayer partners are some of the biggest blessings in my life. I try to have four prayer partners at any given time. This is in addition to my wife and children, who are certainly partners in prayer as well. But why *four* prayer partners? I have specifically chosen four, based on the model of the New Testament characters of Paul, Barnabas, Timothy, and Lydia.

My "Paul" prayer partner is a mentor. This is someone who is older and wiser than I am. (The wiser part is easy... The older part is getting trickier!) My "Paul" is someone who can tell me the brutally honest truth, even when I might not want to hear it. We all need a "Paul" who can set us straight when we start to wander off the path – someone who will always speak the truth in love even when it's a hard truth.

My "Barnabas" prayer partner is a peer encourager. The name Barnabas actually means "son of encouragement." (Barnabas in the Scriptures was actually named Joseph, but they changed his name when they realized his gift of encouragement! By the way, what should we change *your* name to?) My Barnabas is someone who is similar in age and has about the same number of years of experience as I do. This is someone who will say my ideas are "interesting," no matter how crazy they might be, and they help me focus on the parts that really are worth developing further. They do not lie. They speak the truth in love, with an emphasis on love. We all need someone who can be a positive and consistent source of encouragement.

My "Timothy" prayer partner is someone whom I am mentoring. This might be someone who is just getting started in the same career as you, and someone that you can serve as a "Paul" prayer partner for! Hopefully this is someone you can inspire – someone to whom you can say, "Don't let anyone look down on you because you are young, but set an example for the believers in speech, in conduct, in love, in faith and in purity" (1 Timothy 4:12) – just as St. Paul said to Timothy.

Lydia may be an unfamiliar biblical character to you, but she was crucial to St. Paul and his mission work. We meet her in Acts 16:14-15:

> One of those listening was a woman from the city of Thyatira named Lydia, a dealer in purple cloth. She was a worshiper of God. The Lord opened her heart to respond to Paul's message. When she and the members of her household were baptized, she invited us to her home. "If you consider me a believer in the Lord," she said, "come and stay at my house." And she persuaded us.

Lydia is a businesswoman – and since she sold purple cloth, it's safe to assume from the cultural context that she was very wealthy. Most theologians believe that Lydia was key in financially supporting Paul's missionary work. My Lydia prayer partner is someone who can provide help through financial support and resources for the ministry. This is someone who has means or who has connections to means. As missionaries, we all need those who can help support our missionary work in financial ways.

This model of having four prayer partners works well because it reminds us how important it is not only to receive help and guidance from others, but also to pass it on to those who need it from *us*! And each of these four individuals is a blessing to my spiritual life in different ways. It would be impossible to find just one person who could fulfill all those roles. However, if you are new to the whole idea of prayer partners, don't feel that you need to go out and find four of them right off the bat. Focus on finding just one trusted partner to start with – someone you feel completely comfortable with. In time, you can branch out with more. These close, deep, trusted relationships take time to build, and quality is always more important than quantity.[1]

Investigative Questions:

1) Do you already have prayer partners in your life?

2) Who would make a good "Paul" in your life?

3) Who would make a good "Barnabas" in your life?

4) Who would make a good "Timothy" in your life?

5) Who would make a good "Lydia" in your life?

Action Item:

Talk to one person about being a prayer partner. Why did you choose that person? How might they help you the most? And how can you, in turn, be a strength and a blessing to *them*?

Chapter 4
I: Individual

All by Myself… with Jesus

While corporate worship is about large community and small group is about intimate community, the "I" in C.S.I. is about the smallest party possible: a party of one – the individual. Or more accurately – the "I" is about you and Jesus, one-on-one. This includes your personal and private prayer, meditation, and study time, alone with God.

Can you imagine what it was like for Adam during his prayer time? He could have conversations with God as they walked through the garden together. What beautiful intimate time that must have been! Adam knew that God knew everything, and yet Adam still talked and shared with Him. In fact, the Genesis account doesn't even refer to Adam talking to God as prayer – it's just talking. It's just part of the relationship, being in conversation.

With the Fall into sin, we have lost that sense of communicative relationship, and I will confess that many times prayer feels awkward. It feels silly at times to tell God things He already knows. It feels odd to ask for the things that I want and need because I know He knows these things better than I do!

Yet, God commands His followers to come to Him in prayer. Prayer is more than just a command – it's a gift. Prayer allows us to articulate our thoughts and feelings, and in so doing a miracle of sorts happens as we understand them better.

Prayer is power. Prayer changes things. Prayer allows us to enter into the same intimacy that Adam had pre-Fall.

Notice throughout the Gospels how much time Jesus spends praying alone. It's His source of strength. He needs one-on-one time with His heavenly Father, and so do you! Pastor Bill Hybells wrote a book called *Too Busy Not to Pray*. The title alone is worth remembering and taking to heart. The busier and more stressed we are, and the more out of control we feel, the more we need that one-on-one time alone with Jesus. Martin Luther said it this way: "I have so much to do that I shall spend the first three hours in prayer."[1] We don't pray just because we *have* the time; we pray because we *need* the time! Make it a priority for your spiritual and mental health. Think of it as an important appointment that you can't miss – in fact, it just might be the most important appointment of your whole day! If it helps you, you may even want to write it down on your calendar, or set alarm notices on your phone, at least until it becomes a regular habit. There are so many different models and formats for individual prayer and Bible reading – all one has to do is Google the topic and more than enough suggestions will come up. I am going to give you a few examples; this is not meant to be a comprehensive list, but rather a place to help get you started. To be fit for the mission, it's crucial for us to set aside that individual time with Jesus on a daily basis, in addition to the corporate worship and small group time.

The key is to find something that will work for *you*, and something that is sustainable. For example, getting up at 4 AM is not sustainable for me because I hate mornings! But rising early might work well for others. Maybe you're a journal person. Great! Keep a prayer journal and talk to God through your written words. Maybe you're a get-on-your-knees-and-shout-to-God person. Wonderful! Pour out your heart to Him, loudly and boldly. Or maybe you're someone who feels closest to God when you are out in nature. Then pray while you walk, bike, run, or simply sit outside in a quiet and peaceful spot. The important thing here is to choose whatever feels most comfortable and natural for you. Similar to an exercise routine or a diet, if it's not sustainable, you will not reap the long-term blessings.

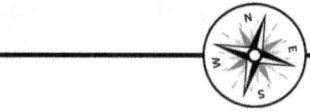

Prayer might be the most important appointment of your whole day!

Interestingly enough, even when we are all alone with just our thoughts, we're never really alone. Jesus promises us in Matthew 28:20, "I am with you always." As Jesus was processing the fact that He would soon suffer and die, He said, "Yet I am not alone, for my Father is with me" (John 16:32). What a great comfort this realization brings us! Jesus is always with us! And what an opportunity it brings. Our "alone" time can be spent intentionally with Jesus. Are you in the car all by yourself? Pray while you drive! (Especially if you are driving on the freeways in Southern California – but that's a different story altogether!) Pray when you are in the shower first thing in the morning, or last thing at night. Pray while you exercise or while you are out walking the dog. Take advantage of those quiet moments in the day when you are alone, and share your thoughts, fears, worries, joys, and needs with God. What an opportunity to connect with your Creator! We are never really alone!

Investigative Questions:

1) How is your Individual spiritual life? Is this something that needs to be a higher priority for you?

2) What specific times during your daily schedule can be used for your quiet time with God?

3) How can your Individual time with Jesus help you answer the question, "Who are you?"

Action Item:

Set a prayer appointment for once a day. What means did you use to remind yourself? How can you make this a regular part of your day? (Is this something your prayer partner can help remind you about?)

Keep Watch!

When Jesus prayed, was He talking to Himself? He is True God, but He's also True Man – which means He's completely dependent on God. Throughout the Gospels, we see examples of Jesus going off by Himself to pray. Let's examine three of these times as found in the Gospel of Mark.

Right away, in the first chapter of Mark, we see that "Very early in the morning, while it was still dark, Jesus got up, left the house and went off to a solitary place, where he prayed. Simon and his companions went to look for him" (Mark 1:35-36). So many details given in the shortest of the Gospel accounts! It's early, and still dark outside, but Jesus needed prayer more than sleep. It was high priority to Him. He left the house and went to a quiet place. In fact, the place was so solitary that His disciples couldn't find Him at first! Jesus greatly valued His alone time with His Father!

In the second account, Mark 6:45-47, we see that

> Immediately Jesus made his disciples get into the boat and go on ahead of him to Bethsaida, while he dismissed the crowd. After leaving them, he went up on a mountainside to pray.
>
> Later that night, the boat was in the middle of the lake, and he was alone on land.

How was Jesus planning to get back in touch with the disciples? No cell phones back then – and it was a far enough journey that they needed a boat! Jesus not only valued prayer time first thing in the morning, but as we see in this account, also late at night. The location of choice this time is a mountain. Why a mountain? He was desiring to be far away from others, but at the same time we know that He's focused on praying *for* others! From the mountain, perhaps He could overlook the city and the people He was praying for. Maybe being up on the mountaintop made Him feel closer to His Father in heaven. Whatever the reason, location matters, or Mark would not have included these details.

The third account of Jesus going off by Himself to pray takes place on the night of His arrest:

> They went to a place called Gethsemane, and Jesus said to his disciples, "Sit here while I pray." He took Peter, James and John along with him, and he began to be deeply distressed and troubled. "My soul is overwhelmed with sorrow to the point of death," he said to them. "Stay here and keep watch."

> Going a little farther, he fell to the ground and prayed that if possible the hour might pass from him. "*Abba*, Father," he said, "everything is possible for you. Take this cup from me. Yet not what I will, but what you will."
>
> Then he returned to his disciples and found them sleeping. "Simon," he said to Peter, "are you asleep? Couldn't you keep watch for one hour? Watch and pray so that you will not fall into temptation. The spirit is willing, but the flesh is weak."
>
> Once more he went away and prayed the same thing. When he came back, he again found them sleeping, because their eyes were heavy. They did not know what to say to him. (Mark 14:32-40)

I used to save most of my prayers for bedtime. While I still value praying as I fall asleep, it's difficult to pray when I'm *actually* asleep! If our only prayer time takes place when we are exhausted, we will not be able to truly focus on the conversation. Jesus says, "Keep watch." That is an important idea in prayer. We pray, and then watch and listen for God's response. Prayer is not just talking, but also listening. Being exhausted at night, or distracted during the day, inhibits us from hearing what God has to say to us.

Here's another point to think about. What do you think Jesus spent most of His time praying about? Do you think He was praying mostly about His own problems and issues? We know that praying for other people was a high priority for Jesus – shouldn't it be for us, too? Andy Stanley says that you can tell what a church's values are from their prayer requests.[1] If the corporate worshiping church is lifting up prayers only for members, that says something. If the church is lifting up prayers only for outsiders to come to knowledge of Jesus, that says something. Prayer just might have the power to live in the tension of missions and discipleship like nothing else!

I would argue the same is true for the individual. Your prayer requests reveal your values. Does your prayer life reflect the values of a Missionary Disciple? Jesus' prayers certainly revealed His values! Prayer requests are revealing in all three aspects of C.S.I.

We could easily spend our whole prayer time giving God all our wants, needs, gripes, and complaints, and never move beyond ourselves and our own situations. But intercessory prayer – praying on behalf of others – is powerful stuff! We have the wonderful privilege of lifting up the needs and concerns of our family, friends, neighbors – everyone – to God, and watching Him work amazing things in their lives. Praying for other people also helps us empathize with them. It's hard to stay angry or resentful toward someone you are actively praying for!

Think, too, how individual prayer connects you to the "C" and "S" in C.S.I. In your individual prayer, you have the opportunity to lift up the requests of the corporate Body of Christ and your intimate small group. If you are not sure what to pray for, I would encourage you to start by asking the people in your church or small group – I am sure they will give you a list of requests.

Investigative Questions:

1) Why do you think Jesus needed "alone" time with His Father?

2) Do you think the times of day when Jesus prayed were significant? How?

3) Do you think the locations where Jesus prayed were significant? How?

4) In thinking about your own alone time with God, do you think it is important when and where you pray?

5) What does "Keep watch" mean to you in regards to prayer? How do you listen to God?

Action Item:

Make a list of prayer requests. What does your list reveal about your identity, mission, and purpose? Who can you share that list with? Ask others to share their lists with you as well.

How's Your Spiritual Health?

At the end of Luke chapter 2, we see an adolescent Jesus who is reunited with His mother after being separated following the Passover celebration. Chapter 2 starts with Jesus' birth, and ends with this line: "Jesus grew in wisdom and stature, and in favor with God and man." As we look at our own individual personal growth and wholeness, this verse is very insightful. A proper understanding of this verse will filter into every aspect of C.S.I. and being a Missionary Disciple.

Jesus grew. He grew like every other human being. But Jesus grew *intentionally*. He grew in wisdom, or *intellectually*. Jesus grew is stature, or *physically*. He grew in favor with God, or *spiritually*, and He grew in favor with man (people), or *socially*. If this is how Jesus grew, what a great model this is for us!

What does it mean to grow intellectually? St. Paul says in 1 Corinthians 13:11, "When I was a child, I talked like a child, I thought like a child, I reasoned like a child. When I became a man, I put the ways of childhood behind me." Growing intellectually is about being a lifelong learner. Gandhi is believed to have said, "Live as if you were to die tomorrow. Learn as if you were to live forever."[1] While I am a huge supporter of traditional schooling, and encourage everyone to continue their education, learning and growing intellectually involve so much more than what is taught in school.

We learn from observing and processing. We learn from reading a book or watching a film. We learn from experience. Research suggests that the best way to learn something is to teach it to others! However you prefer to learn, never stop growing intellectually. There is an ancient Chinese proverb that says, "If you want to plan for one year, plant rice. If you want to plan for ten years, plant trees. If you want to plan for one hundred years, educate."[2] Learning can be difficult and frustrating, but to stop learning is to stop living.

What does it mean to grow physically? Growth is a natural part of life, but I am talking about a physical growth beyond height – and even beyond width… It also means taking good care of your body. St. Paul says in 1 Corinthians 6:19-20, "Do you not know that your bodies are temples of the Holy Spirit, who is in you, whom you have received from God? You are not your own; you were bought at a price. Therefore honor God with your bodies." To be the Missionary Disciple God has dreamed us to be, we need to take adequate care of our bodies. For most of us, there's still room for improvement in this area! High cholesterol runs in my family, and my doctor has told me that there are three keys to a physically healthy lifestyle: diet, exercise, and sleep.

If you have ever seen a late-night infomercial, then you know that humanity is always searching for quick fixes and shortcuts to these three principles of diet, exercise, and sleep. We've all heard the claims: *Buy these pills and lose weight easily and without exercise!* Or: *This pill will help you sleep soundly every night – and it's non-habit-forming!* And have you seen the fast-food commercials that show super-skinny models eating large greasy hamburgers? Unfortunately, that is not how life works. Diet, exercise, and sleep take discipline and consistency. There are no shortcuts. Paraphrasing a line from the U.S. Army, we cannot *be all that we can be* unless we take care of ourselves physically. Most importantly, you cannot be all that *God* has dreamed you to be unless you take care of your physical being.

What does it mean to grow spiritually? When God came to Solomon in a dream and offered him anything his heart desired, Solomon said this:

> You have shown great kindness to your servant, my father David, because he was faithful to you and righteous and upright in heart. You have continued this great kindness to him and have given him a son to sit on his throne this very day.
>
> Now, LORD my God, you have made your servant king in place of my father David. But I am only a little

child and do not know how to carry out my duties. Your servant is here among the people you have chosen, a great people, too numerous to count or number. So give your servant a discerning heart to govern your people and to distinguish between right and wrong. (1 Kings 3:6-9)

Solomon could have asked for anything, but what did he ask for? A discerning heart. This – what I refer to as a healthy spiritual heart – is the key to spiritual growth. Let's apply what we know about the physical heart to the spiritual heart – that to be healthy, we need to embrace diet, exercise, and sleep.

What is our spiritual diet? Jesus said it best when Satan tried to tempt Him to turn rocks into loaves of bread: "Man shall not live on bread alone, but on every word that comes from the mouth of God" (Matthew 4:4). Our spiritual diet is God's Word! We are to treat God's Word as food – digest it, internalize it, and grow from it, to the benefit of our health and well-being. What happens when we neglect the Word and instead consume a lot of junk? We become spiritually weak, and we are less able to handle the demands of life.

What is our spiritual exercise? In James 1:27, we learn that "Religion that God our Father accepts as pure and faultless is this: to look after orphans and widows in their distress and to keep oneself from being polluted by the world." Our spiritual exercise is our mission and service. It's loving "the least of these" (Matthew 25:40). When we are focused on the things of God, we naturally grow closer to God. Mission is our spiritual exercise.

In my work with the church in Tanzania, I've been incredibly impressed with their ministry to widows and orphans who are truly the outcasts in that society. The church sponsors a program for widows where they are taught basic job skills, and assists them in finding jobs. The church runs several orphanages – some focusing on Albino Tanzanian kids who are truly the lowest of the low in that culture. The church educates them, teaches them the Gospel, helps to find caring homes for them, and otherwise assists them in becoming contributing members of society. The church in Tanzania gets the Missionary Disciple concept!

Mission is our spiritual exercise

What is our spiritual equivalent of sleep? God calls it Sabbath. We rest in Him. Remembering the Sabbath day certainly includes a regular worship experience, but it's also about resting in the presence of the Creator. When we rest in Him, He renews our body, mind, and soul. It seems like we live in a world of perpetual motion. From the moment we get up in the morning till the moment our head hits the pillow at night, we are always running around, always busy doing *something*. But God invites us to put everything else aside for a while and come be with Him. And not only on Sundays! It is important to prioritize time to be still and rest in God every single day of the week! The book *Subversive Sabbath* has helped me really refocus my understanding of Sabbath: "Sabbath is a foretaste of Heaven!"[3]

There are no shortcuts to spiritual growth, just as there are no shortcuts to physical growth. The magic pill or fad diet will only lead to unhealthy living. We have to be regularly disciplined to be a Missionary Disciple.

And finally, what does it mean to grow socially? While physical, mental, and spiritual connect to the human trinity (heart, mind, and soul) we talked about in a previous chapter – this social idea is where it all comes together. We know that it is not good to live in isolation (Genesis 2:18). We need others – and just as importantly, other people need us! We were designed for community. We are better together. To grow in favor with man (people) is to obey the second half of The Great Commandment, "Love your neighbor as yourself" (Matthew 22:39). We grow socially when we love others – which is missions!

But the part of this text that we often skip over when teaching The Great Commandment is Matthew 22:40 – "All the Law and the Prophets hang on these two commandments." By stating "All the Law and the Prophets," Jesus is saying that all of society should be built upon these commandments. Without loving your neighbor, there is no civility, and civilization itself falls apart. To grow socially, we strive to love with a genuine, honest, true, unconditional love. By God's grace, our wholeness in body, mind, and soul leads to society's wholeness. Our wholeness in our identity as a disciple leads to a desire to be on mission to bring about society's wholeness.

Investigative Questions:

1) What does it mean to you to grow intellectually? Physically? Spiritually? Socially?

2) What shortcuts have you been taking lately in these four areas? How can you improve?

3) How do you think diet, exercise, and sleep affect your heart, mind, and soul?

Action Item:

- Write down one way you want to grow intellectually:

- Write down one way you want to grow physically:

- Write down one way you want to grow spiritually:

- Write down one way you want to grow socially:

- Looking back over them, do these growth areas appear to be challenging? Who could help you in these growth areas?

Ideas for You to Investigate

Eating the Scroll

The prophet Ezekiel would have made a great youth minister because he loved a good object lesson. He was not afraid to use everything from a haircut to "poop" to make God's words clear and understandable. In Ezekiel chapter 3, he literally eats a scroll containing God's Word. I know what you're thinking – "Did it taste like chicken?" The account says that it actually tasted like honey! The point of the story: God's Word needs to be internalized! It needs to live in us to work through us.

One of my students once told me, "When I'm in the Word personally, I'm a better teacher of the Word." *Exactly!* Each of us needs to be in the Word personally on a daily basis. It's our food. If we skip a meal, we are not going to be as strong and healthy. The Word of God needs to be internalized, meaning that it becomes a part of us. God says this in Deuteronomy:

> Fix these words of mine in your hearts and minds; tie them as symbols on your hands and bind them on your foreheads. Teach them to your children, talking about them when you sit at home and when you walk along the road, when you lie down and when you get up. Write them on the doorframes of your houses and on your gates, so that your days and the days of your children may be many in the land the LORD swore to give your ancestors, as many as the days that the heavens are above the earth. (Deuteronomy 11:18-21)

The Word of God needs to be a part of us. And when it is, eternity lives inside of us!

But how do we internalize the Word of God in us? Below I give a few suggestions to try:

Read the Bible every year, cover to cover. There are a wide variety of reading plans to guide you through this.[1] Reading plans can be done from cover to cover – from Genesis to Revelation – straight through the Bible. There are also chronological reading plans where you read the Bible through the narrative timeline. Or you can choose a reading plan where you read through the Bible by the historical dates based on when they were written. No matter which plan you choose, the key is to pick a plan and commit to it!

If you are new to the story of Jesus, I highly recommend that you start with the book of Mark. I recommend this simply because Mark is the shortest of the Gospels, and gives us a great picture of the life and times of Jesus. Mark was a close friend of Peter, one of the original twelve disciples of Jesus, and most scholars believe that Mark assembled his Gospel from the preaching he heard from Peter – which makes it an eyewitness account! Mark is Barnabas's cousin and also spent time doing missionary work with St. Paul, so Mark understands the fervor with which the Gospel needs to be presented. He understands what it means to be a Missionary Disciple. Mark is a great place to start the Jesus story.

Proverbs is a collection of the wisdom of King Solomon. Interestingly enough, Proverbs has 31 chapters. You could read one chapter a day for a month! (February will mess you up a bit, but you'll figure it out.) Martin Luther said, "Proverbs may properly be called a book of good works, for in it he teaches how to lead a good life before God and the world."[2] Proverbs is not a story; however, you will see that the wisdom presented connects to your own story, and it will help you live a fuller life.

The Psalms are the biblical prayer and song book. Read one each morning and reflect on it, asking God to show you how to apply it throughout your day. As you read through the Psalms, you might be led to sing aloud. The Psalms are used to provide lyrics and inspiration for many of the most popular hymns, praise choruses, and songs.

Here's another great tool for spending time in the Word: Download an audio Bible or get a Bible app for your phone.[3] Then you can listen in the car, at the gym, while out for a run, as you fall asleep at night, or wherever you can't easily read text. And since we are reminded that faith comes by hearing (Romans 10:17), listening to the Scriptures can be a powerful way to internalize them.

Also, take note that in this section I did not recommend any additional books to aid you in your Bible study. Commentaries are good, and there are so many other incredible books that will help you understand and grow in your faith (you might even be reading one right now!). But all of these extras are just that – extras. First and foremost, we need to dig into and internalize the actual Bible. Reading a book about the Word of God is not a substitute for reading the Word itself, in all its purity. It is important to allow the Word of God to speak to us in a unique and personal way.

Investigative Questions:

1) What is your favorite verse or passage? Favorite book of the Bible? How do these speak to you?

2) What will your personal reading plan look like? What appeals to you about this plan?

3) What does it mean to you to "internalize" the Scriptures? How can you do more of this?

Action Item:

Read through the book of Mark. Try to do it in one sitting or large chunks at a time, to get the fullness of the story. What are some new things you noticed? Have someone read it aloud with you to get a fuller experience.[4]

Writing Loudly

Did you realize that there is only one Scriptural account of Jesus writing anything down? I've always wondered why there aren't more. We know He could read, but for some reason we don't hear about Him doing much writing. The only hint we have is in John 8, where He is brought before a woman who has committed adultery – and the authorities try to trap Him, asking what they should do with her. The account then says, "Jesus bent down and started to write on the ground with his finger" (v. 6). What was He writing? Wouldn't we love to know!

Journaling is telling our story through the lens of God's story

During a recent sabbatical, I developed a new appreciation for daily journaling. I journaled every day for six months. My previous personal record was no more than a week. There is great power in writing out your thoughts and prayers. It helps you internalize them, and gives you the ability to reflect back on them later. Looking back at previous entries, you can see all the ways in which your prayers were answered, and how your faith has grown and developed through all the ups and downs you've gone through. You can recognize pieces to the puzzle that now make sense in hindsight.

When asked about writing down his thoughts, St. Augustine said:

> Why, then, do I set before You an ordered account of so many things? It's certainly not through me that You know them. But I'm stirring up love for You in myself and in those who read this so that we may all say, great is the Lord and highly worthy to be praised. I tell my story for love of Your love.[1]

I love the idea of "I tell my story for love of Your love"! Journaling is telling our story through the lens of God's story. What a great reason to keep a prayer journal!

Paper or digital? Some people like to use a journaling app on their phone or tablet to write down their entries, while others enjoy the feeling of putting ink to paper in a spiral notebook or a blank journal. Choose whichever is more comfortable for you.

I also want to add a note here about privacy. At least initially, your journal should be a safe, personal place where you can feel free to bring any thoughts, feelings, and concerns you may have to God. If you are worried about other people possibly reading what you write, you might want to consider using a digital journaling method that can be password-protected. This will give you the peace of mind and freedom to write anything you wish.

But at the same time, reread the St. Augustine quote a few paragraphs above. Our prayer journal just might be used by others to see God's love. As I look back at some of my prayer journals, certain things I previously considered extremely private when they were first written have since been read aloud in class or shared with a friend years later to show how God has worked in my life.

Don't know where to start in keeping a prayer journal? Here are a few ideas and outlines:

1) **S.O.A.P.**: Soap cleans. But it has to be used! If you just set your bar of soap on your coffee table, you might impress your friends with your perceived cleanliness. But to really be clean, you have to *use* the soap. Soap is a powerful metaphor for us and for the cleaning work that God desires to do through us and in us:

    S: Scripture – Type or handwrite the verse or verses that stick out to you in your daily Bible reading. No copying and pasting blocks of text! Writing it out helps you to internalize it and think through every single word.

    O: Observation – What did you observe about the Scripture that struck you? This can be one sentence or a whole book.

    A: Application – How can you apply the observation so that it affects your life today?

    P: Prayer – Write a prayer to God based on what you just learned, and ask Him to help you apply this truth in your life.

2) **P.A.R.T.**: Another model of prayer and journaling is found in the word *PART*. What I like about this word is the reminder of the "part" that God plays – and the part that I play – in our prayer relationship.

> **P**: Praise – Praise God for who He is and what He has done. A Psalm fits very nicely here as well, or perhaps a song that has been stuck in your head. God is truly worthy of our praise. Praise Him!
>
> **A**: Admit – This is your confession time. Admit your sins, trusting in His mercy and grace to forgive them all. Cling to His promises of forgiveness, and know that He removes your sin as far as the east is from the west! (cf. Psalm 103:12)
>
> **R**: Request – What do you want from God? Tell Him your wants, needs, and desires, knowing that He will listen. When requesting, know that God's answer will sometimes be *yes*, and sometimes *no*. But He will always answer! Explore the reasons and things He longs to teach you when He answers *yes* or *no*. Sometimes He might be saying, *Wait, you're not ready yet – you need to do some growing first*. Other times He is protecting you from yourself! But make no mistake, He always answers!
>
> **T**: Thanks – What are you thankful for? Perhaps it is in direct response to a request. Perhaps it is a blessing you've received that you did not even think of asking for! Thank the Lord for His act of salvation and for the miracles that you see all around you.

3) Free-flowing method (stream of consciousness) – This method isn't structured, so it may appeal to some people more than others. Just write down your thoughts as they come to you, even if they are jumbled and disorganized, knowing that God understands and hears them all. This method works especially well when many things are weighing heavily upon us, and we just need to do a prayer dump and pour all our concerns and fears and needs out to God. You may find that certain verses of Scripture will then come to mind as you write, giving you strength and comfort for your circumstances.

Whichever method you choose for your prayer journal, I know you will find it to be spiritually rewarding and encouraging!

Investigative Questions:

1) In what specific ways would you benefit from journaling?

2) How could writing help you reflect back?

3) Which model do you prefer? (Or create your own model!)

Action Item:

Journal your prayers for a week – then go back and reread them. What do you notice? What has changed? What have you learned? Is there someone you would be comfortable sharing this with?[2]

When and Where for Prayer

As we think about our individual time with God, the location and the time of day do have significance. Sometimes you might need a quiet spot to truly reflect and gather your thoughts. Maybe you prefer to be out in nature, breathing in the fresh air and getting some vitamin D from the sunlight. There is a little creek that runs behind my house, and hearing that running water while in my individual time constantly reminds me of my baptism.

Sometimes you might feel the need to be around people – in other words, to be alone in the crowd. I have always found the idea of prayer-walking to be powerful. Prayer-walking is when you physically walk through an area or around the people you are praying for. On a trip to New York City, I walked around the perimeter of 843-acre Central Park. About 40 million people visit the park a year, and I felt like I ran into about half that many. I prayed for every person I saw. I didn't get the opportunity to talk to many people besides basic pleasantries. I took in the sights, sounds, and smells of the city as I walked and prayed. It was beautiful! – but a very different beautiful than the little creek in my backyard. Physical proximity facilitates empathizing with others. There are many models for prayer-walking, but just keep it simple: Walk and pray about what you see.

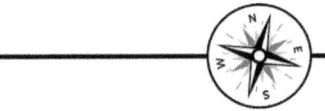

"Pray continually" (1 Thessalonians 5:17).
What would life look like if we actually did?!

On mission trips to Muslim countries, I have grown to admire how they pray. Devote Muslims pray five times a day, and the timing is very significant. The first prayer time, offered before the sun comes up, is a way to remember Allah and thank him for the day that is about to come. During the second prayer, at noon, they take a break from their work and seek Allah's guidance. The third prayer comes in the late afternoon, at the end of the work day, as a time to give thanks for work but also as a reminder that there is more to life than work. The fourth prayer, just after the sun has set, is a time to give thanks for the blessings of the day. The fifth and final prayer of the day comes right before one goes to sleep; this is a prayer of forgiveness and thanks. I will never forget my first time visiting a Muslim country and hearing the loud horns signaling the time for obligatory prayer. Everybody – literally everyone around us, except for my little mission team – got on their knees facing Mecca and prayed.

Can we learn anything from this example? Absolutely! Now, I am not suggesting that we should pray ritually, or out of a sense of obligation. But there are some natural transition times during our day (for example, when we wake up, when we start and end our work/school day, when we go to bed) when we might like to just stop everything for a moment and offer up a prayer to God – asking Him for guidance and wisdom, and thanking Him for the blessings He has given us.

The idea here is to make a more deliberate effort to be thinking about God throughout our day, and remembering that He is the source of everything that we have. When something good happens, could we stop for just a moment and thank God? Would praying over our moments of stress and anxiety provide some relief? When someone is driving us crazy, what if we stopped, took a deep breath, and just prayed for them?

One of the shortest verses in the Bible is 1 Thessalonians 5:17, "Pray continually." What would life look like if we actually did?! Missionary Disciples who are growing and going value continuous prayer.

Tying prayer into certain activities or times of the day is also a great idea if you are one of those people who gets so busy and wrapped up in other things that you often forget to pray. As I mentioned in a previous section, you can always find alone time to pray… while taking a shower, driving to work, riding your bike to class, taking the dog for a walk, etc. Use that time to talk to God. And after a while, you will begin to associate these daily activities with prayer time, so that soon it will become automatic to do them together.

As you think about time and place, I also encourage you to think about *listening* – not just talking. Any true dialogue involves both. We often spend our whole prayer time talking to God, and then we move on with our day without pausing to give Him a chance to communicate back. Setting aside some time just to be still and quiet before God is important, so we can hear what He wants to tell us. What time and what place would make it easier for you to listen to Him?

Investigative Questions:

1) What is your favorite time of day to pray? Why?

2) Where is your favorite place to pray? Why?

3) What can Christians learn from Muslims about prayer? What can Muslims learn from Christians about prayer?

4) How many times a day do you pray? What can you do to increase the frequency of your prayers?

5) What does 1 Thessalonians 5:17 mean to you?

Action Item:

Find a prayer place and time, and use it every day for a week. Were your prayers different? Were you more focused? Ask some of your friends about their favorite prayer times and locations, and if they don't already have a routine for prayer, encourage them to try one.

Posture Matters

One of my favorite experiential prayer lessons to do with a group is to have everyone lay on their stomachs, then get on their knees, then stand with their arms reaching up as high as they can (yes, it feels like prayer-latés!) – and finally, sit with their hands folded, head bowed, and eyes closed. After all of the exercises, I ask them this question: "Which one of these prayer postures is *not* modeled in Scripture?" Almost everyone gets it right. It's the last one – the Scriptures do not speak of folding one's hands. I then ask them, "Which one of these postures do you use most often when you pray?" And almost always, the answer is the last one – hands folded, head bowed, eyes closed.

So why do we pray like that? Where did you first learn to pray in this position? When teaching kids to pray, I used to always say, "Fold your hands, bow your heads, close your eyes, and focus your minds." I guess this was because I wanted them to "behave" during prayer time. But what would happen if we changed our posture?

Let's walk through the three prayer postures that are modeled in Scripture. The first is called *prostrate*, which means to lay down on your belly with your face toward the ground. It's a position of surrender. Moses models this immediately after he discovers the people of God have been worshiping a golden calf. In Deuteronomy 9:18, as Moses is recounting the golden calf story, he says, "Then once again I fell prostrate before the LORD for forty days and forty nights; I ate no bread and drank no water." In a sense, prostrate is a position of complete and absolute surrender. Prostrate is the position of the dead, and the dead are always so good at staying in one position! Good thing that when we lay prostrate before God, He's a God of resurrection!

The second posture that we see modeled in Scripture is on one's knees. This is a position of submission. Daniel (of Daniel and the Lions' Den fame) was commanded by King Darius not to pray to God, but only to pray to the king as "god." But Daniel 6:10 tells us:

> Now when Daniel learned that the decree had been published, he went home to his upstairs room where the windows opened toward Jerusalem. Three times a day he got down on his knees and prayed, giving thanks to his God, just as he had done before.

Daniel was respectful to the king and a good servant to him, but he knew that he could only truly submit to God. And through his submission to God, even though the king sought to take Daniel's life, God saved it!

Lifting up one's hands is a signal of victory. In American football, everyone waits with bated breath for the referee to throw up both hands declaring "touchdown!" The Psalms are full of examples of hands being lifted high. Here are several examples:

- "Hear my cry for mercy as I call to you for help, as I lift up my hands toward your Most Holy Place" (Psalm 28:2).
- "I will praise you as long as I live, and in your name I will lift up my hands" (Psalm 63:4).
- "Lift up your hands in the sanctuary and praise the LORD" (Psalm 134:2).

The people of God have much to celebrate! We celebrate the victories of God, and we celebrate with each other. As St. Paul says in 1 Timothy 2:8, "I want the men everywhere to pray, lifting up holy hands without anger or disputing." When one is busy praising and celebrating, it is difficult to be involved in anger or disputing!

Interestingly, raising one's hands in the air is also a signal of surrender. Surrender and celebration is yet another paradox. And yet, it just might be the best image of what prayer is: a celebration of what God is doing and a surrendering to His will.

Have you ever thought about your prayer posture before? If you feel that your prayer life is in a rut, perhaps a change of posture could help. It might make more of a difference than you'd think. If our postures during prayer were not important, why would so many people in the Scriptures model them for us?

Investigative Questions:

1) What posture do you use normally when you pray? Why? Where did you learn it?

2) When would you want to pray prostrate?

3) When would you prefer to pray on your knees?

4) What circumstances might make you want to pray with your hands lifted high?

Action Item:

Try all three biblical prayer postures for a few days. How do they affect your prayer life?

Go Away!

Our world is so busy, stressful, and confusing! Do you ever just want to escape for a while and recharge, emotionally and spiritually? Then consider all the benefits of a personal retreat. Imagine… 24 hours of nothing but resting in the presence of God. For this idea to really work, the most important thing is to eliminate distractions, which means – you guessed it – no electronics! No cell phone, no iPad, no Netflix. In fact, I would suggest you only take a Bible, a note pad, pen, water, and some food.

Your two best friends on your personal retreat will be peace and solitude. In Mark 6 we see the disciples of Jesus on the verge of burnout. They had been so busy that they did not even have a chance to eat (Mark 6:31a)! Jesus' response to their busyness was, "Come with me by yourselves to a quiet place and get some rest" (Mark 6:31b).

"Come with me by yourselves" is what the "I" in C.S.I. is all about. Just you and Jesus, one-on-one. No distractions. No other people. This is what solitude means. I will admit that solitude is difficult for me because I'm extremely extroverted! I come from a big family. I'm blessed with many great friends and neighbors. I love being around people, and I thrive on it. But I have learned that in my solitude, I can connect to Jesus in a unique and personal way. Solitude allows us to hear the "gentle whisper" (1 Kings 19:12) of God. The prophet Elijah learned this the hard way in 1 Kings 19. Solitude may not feel natural for you at first, but the blessings are limitless.

Your "quiet place" is not about finding complete silence as much as a peaceful place with no distractions. For example, nature noises might be peaceful for you. The sound of waves crashing or a brook bubbling can be meditative and a reminder of the promises given through baptism. Or for those who are more indoors people, the gentle turning of a ceiling fan or hum of the air conditioner can be peaceful and a reminder of God's provisions. Or for me, sometimes my quiet place in a noisy airport or airplane is with my noise-canceling headphones on and a favorite podcast playing. Close your eyes right now.

What do you hear? The key is not absence of sound, but clarity of thought and absence of distractions.

Mark 6 also demonstrates for us the resulting blessing of peace and solitude: rest. In our individual time, Jesus gives us rest. Even God rested on the seventh day of creation. He did so to model for us the way that we should live. We are called to live a life of creative and meaningful work, but also to set aside regular times of rest. We *need* rest. In fact, we need it so much that God even commands us to rest in the Ten Commandments. Exodus 20:8-11 says:

> Remember the Sabbath day by keeping it holy. Six days you shall labor and do all your work, but the seventh day is a Sabbath to the LORD your God. On it you shall not do any work, neither you, nor your son or daughter, nor your male or female servant, nor your animals, nor any foreigner residing in your towns. For in six days the LORD made the heavens and the earth, the sea, and all that is in them, but he rested on the seventh day. Therefore the LORD blessed the Sabbath day and made it holy.

Have you ever noticed that well-meaning Christians (including some pastors and church workers) will sometimes brag about breaking the Third Commandment? "I'm so busy – I haven't had a day off in a month!" Translation: *I am so important that my workplace will fall apart without me.* One pastor actually told me, "The devil doesn't take a day off, so why should I?" I'm not sure it's ever a good idea to compare our work habits to the devil's!

Funny, isn't it – we don't brag about breaking any other commandments, do we? No one says, "I have presented a false witness against my neighbor ten times this week! I'm so important!" Or, "I have completely dishonored my mother and father this week – it's been the best week ever!" (OK, maybe teenagers do this… but that's a part of adolescence!) In fact, breaking the other nine commandments in some cases will get you fired. But breaking the Sabbath commandment just might get you promoted! Sadly, our society today often rewards and encourages excess.

"Come with me by yourselves" is what the "I" in C.S.I. is all about

---

We need our restful times of peace and solitude, as God has intended for us. A personal retreat is a great way to honor the Sabbath day and keep it holy. Hear the words of Jesus again: "Come with me by yourselves to a quiet place and get some rest." What a powerful promise!

You may be thinking, *Wow, 24 hours is a long time to go without any electronics or other stuff to do! What if I get bored?*[1] If that's the case, you might want to plan ahead for what you will be doing during your retreat time. Here are just a few ideas:

- Choose a book of the Bible to read and reflect on. Write down your thoughts, questions, and insights as you read.
- Write down everything that is weighing heavily upon you – all your concerns, worries, fears, etc. – and bring each one to God. Take time to listen to what He has to say!
- Remember all the times when you told someone, "I'll pray for you!" – and then you forgot? Take some time to really pray earnestly for other people, especially those you haven't included in your prayers in a while.
- Write out all your personal and professional goals for the coming weeks and months, and maybe even years. Lift each one up to God and ask for His direction, guidance, and blessing.
- Sing some of your favorite Christian songs and hymns, and reflect on their meaning. If you play an instrument, you may want to bring it along!
- Set aside time for gratitude. Thank God for all that you are, all that you have, all the opportunities and resources that He has blessed you with – especially the things you sometimes take for granted.
- Make a list of all your spiritual gifts, special talents, and skills. Ask God to give you opportunities to use each one, and to be a blessing to others and to God's kingdom.

If it's hard for you to commit to 24 hours, start with a few hours. Maybe a full-day personal retreat is not plausible right now, so start smaller. What about a two-hour retreat? Two hours is basically the length of a movie. Think small steps.

For my personal retreats, being outdoors is the key. I love to go for long hikes with a backpack full of snacks, water, my

Bible, and a journal. I am always amazed how even in the middle of a metropolitan area, it does not take long to find a hike where you will not see another human being for hours.

During this time, I have a set Scripture reading plan. I might even listen to a podcast or two during the day. I'll spend long periods of time in prayer where I am just talking to God – sometimes out loud, as if He's walking beside me.

These are always times of refreshment for me. They recharge me. I'm an extreme extrovert who loves being around people, and it took me quite a while to get comfortable with it – but personal retreats are life-giving and recharging. So often we focus on quality time with God in our prayer and in the Word, but through a personal retreat you get to spend *quantity* time with Him as well.

Investigative Questions:

1) What do peace and solitude look like for you?

2) What does it mean for you to remember the Sabbath day?

3) What will it take for you to schedule a personal retreat?

Action Item:

This month, plan a minimum 2½-hour personal retreat. Think of it as a "tithe" of one day's time. Start there, and see where it goes!

Chapter 5
Going as We're Growing

Avengers: End Game wraps up 11 years and 22 movies (3,000 minutes!) of cinematic storytelling.[1] As the title alludes to, it is the end. At the risk of giving major spoilers, it's the end specifically for the iconic comic book characters Captain America and Iron Man. Both of their stories end in beautifully satisfying ways – mostly due to two factors: First, they never had it all figured out. Second, they grew throughout their journeys.

You will never have it all figured out – and yet the call is to *go*. If you wait until you know everything, you will never go. When you go, you will grow. There is no teacher quite like experience. God's truths empower you to go, cause you to grow, come alive when you go, and become more tangible as you grow.

I treasure sitting down with my seniors the night before Placement Day. Placement Day is the day when the world finds out where they are going for their DCE (Director of Christian Education) internship. Some are going down the road, and some are going around the world. Some just get in their car and drive, and some need to sell their car in preparation for moving far away. The first question I have for all of them during this time is, "When you think about your new ministry, what terrifies you and what excites you?"

This might seem like an odd question, but I need them to be excited – because they have been working and preparing for this moment for years. This is a call from God, and there is nothing in life more exciting than fulfilling a call from God!

And I also need them to be terrified, because this is a spiritual battle. Following Jesus is difficult. Satan is going to do whatever he can to make their lives miserable. I need them to know they still have a lot to learn. I need them to be comfortable living in this tension of terrified and excited. Ministry is the best job in the world, but it's also the hardest job in the world! I need them to know that you grow as you go, and you go as you grow.

What I really love about Iron Man's story is the transformation from selfish to self-sacrificing. He gave his life for his friends. His journey was never easy. He made major mistakes and suffered countless loses, and yet he grew throughout his journey – and that growth led to complete transformation.

Captain America's story also came full circle but in a very different way. Steve Rodgers became Captain America because of his selfless nature. He loved to serve! He gave everything he had in that service, and once he realizes that the world is safe, he allows himself to have a life of his own and to serve his family. He would not have been able to serve his family well if he didn't follow his mission first. He grows as he goes. You can see him embrace the idea of "Well done, good and faithful servant" (Matthew 25:21). Every journey is different – and every journey is about going and growing.

As we explore going and growing, I want to take you through Acts chapter 1, where St. Luke walks us through the Ascension account again before he gets into the acts of the Apostles. Jesus says in Acts 1:8, "You will be my witnesses in

Chapter 5 – Going as We're Growing

Jerusalem, and in all Judea and Samaria, and to the ends of the earth." As with all of Jesus' words, I believe He chose those words – those geographical locations – very specifically.

Before we get into geography, though, let's focus on the word "witness." Jesus tells us that we will be His witnesses. Eyewitnesses today are not always known for their reliability in court, but in an ancient Jewish court of law, they were very significant. They were crucial to the entire case; in fact there was no case without them!

Deuteronomy 19:15, written thousands of years before Jesus but still followed strictly in the days of Jesus, tells us, "One witness is not enough to convict anyone accused of any crime or offense they may have committed. A matter must be established by the testimony of two or three witnesses." Witnesses were key to the Jewish court system. Witnesses were the proof required to convict someone, and one witness was not enough – there needed to be two or three. So when Jesus says we are His witnesses, He is saying that we are proof! We are the proof that He exists, that He loves, that He saves, that He lives, and that He's coming to take us home. Being proof of something is a major responsibility!

View Matthew 16:13-17 through the lens of "witnesses":

> When Jesus came to the region of Caesarea Philippi, he asked his disciples, "Who do people say the Son of Man is?"
>
> They replied, "Some say John the Baptist; others say Elijah; and still others, Jeremiah or one of the prophets."

"But what about you?" he asked. "Who do you say I am?"

Simon Peter answered, "You are the Messiah, the Son of the living God."

Jesus replied, "Blessed are you, Simon son of Jonah, for this was not revealed to you by flesh and blood, but by my Father in heaven."

Jesus is preparing them to be eyewitnesses! He's showing them what it means to be "proof." He's teaching them to avoid the distractions and lies of the world, and focus on the truth. I believe that the question, "Who do you say Jesus is?" is at the heart of being missional. If you haven't wrestled with this question before, then today's the day! Our words – and perhaps most importantly, our lives and how we travel through the trials and realities of life – communicate that Jesus is the Messiah, the Savior of the world! Being a proven witness is a huge responsibility, and also an incredible opportunity to make sure people know the truth!

Now go back to the specific geographical locations. Jesus mentions Jerusalem, Judea, Samaria, and the Ends of the Earth. Some have argued that Jesus wants this to be a progression, like a ladder where you just keep going up and up until you reach the top. But Jesus does not say Jerusalem, *then* Judea, *then* Samaria, *then* the Ends of the Earth. Others have argued that this is a list of "options," like a multiple-choice quiz, and one simply needs to pick an answer and stick with it. But it doesn't say Jerusalem, *or* Judea, *or* Samaria, *or* the Ends of the Earth.

Chapter 5 – Going as We're Growing   145

I would argue that it's all-inclusive. It *has* to be all-inclusive. We're called to be witnesses, proof, or missionaries in Jerusalem, *and* in Judea, *and* in Samaria, *and* to the Ends of the Earth. Everywhere! That's the missional life! Viewing the entire world – home, near, and far – as the mission field, viewing every human encounter and relationship as an opportunity to share the Gospel!

You will never have it all figured out –
and yet the call is to go.

Some have argued that Jerusalem, and Judea, and Samaria, and the Ends of the Earth would be convertible to city, state, country, and world in today's context, but as we look closely at these specific geographical locations, some additional ideas arise. Jerusalem was the Holy City. It's where the "in crowd," the Jew's Jew, lived. In the Old Testament book of Nehemiah we are reminded of the importance of the Holy City, and Nehemiah leads the charge to rebuild the walls around the city to protect those inside and keep out those who mean to do harm. It's a safe place, a sanctuary from the cruelty of the outside world. I like to view my "Jerusalem" as my local church – people who already know Jesus as their Lord and Savior. We can be missional with Christians too!

I get to visit a wide variety of churches in my current role at Concordia University Texas. Many of the churches I visit have a sign at the parking lot exit that reads: *You Are Now Entering the Mission Field.* Maybe your church has this sign. But at one church I visited, the sign was placed on both sides of the sign pole – and as people drive into the church parking lot, they are reminded that the church building and property are a mission field as well! So the question is: *How can I be a witness to people in and at my church?*

Judea is a much bigger area geographically, but they were still recognized as the pure, true, chosen people of Israel. Judah was one of the twelve original tribes of Israel, named after one of the patriarch Jacob's sons. All of southern Israel eventually became known as the Kingdom of Judea.

I think we can view our "Judea" as people in our community who are "like" us. Maybe they have the same socioeconomic status. Maybe they have similar ethnic or cultural backgrounds. These are people in our community who would feel comfortable walking into our church but, for whatever reason, are not connected to our church yet. *How can I be a witness to the people in my community who are like me?*

Samaria is the name given to the Northern Kingdom. And in Jesus' time, they were viewed very harshly by the good Jewish people. They were not "pure Jews" – they were essentially half Jew and half Assyrian. Their hybrid status put them on par with the Gentiles. They were hated and despised by the Jews, which made Jesus' encounter with a Samaritan women in John chapter 4 so powerful – as well as His parable about the "Good Samaritan" (Luke chapter 10). We can view our "Samaria" as people in our community who are *not* like us.

Maybe they have significantly less or more means than we do. Maybe they have a different color skin. Maybe they speak a different language. Odds are if they walked into your church, they would not feel comfortable at first. *How can I be a witness to people who are not like me?*

"Ends of the Earth" seems rather self-explanatory, but let's explain it anyway. Anywhere on the planet that contains human beings needs a witness who can speak their language, love them for who they are, and share the grace, mercy, and love we have in Jesus! The Ends of the Earth could be at the end of your street, or it could be halfway around the world, but the call is to be His witnesses to the Ends of the Earth. *How can I be a witness to the Ends of the Earth?*[2]

May we be growing and going through Jerusalem, and Judea, and Samaria, and to the Ends of the Earth!

Chapter 6
Not a Tame God

While on safari in Tanzania, my family and I got way too close to a cheetah. Basically, we were minding our own business when a cheetah decided to jump on top of our open jeep and put his paw – complete with razor-sharp, inch-long claws – a few feet from our youngest daughter's head. He sat there and just stared at us. We all just froze, unsure what to do – but seeing the blood from a recent kill dripping off its face, we knew things could get dangerous quickly. Our guide was assuring us that everything was going to be fine – and to prove it, he started taking a selfie with the cheetah – then, the next thing you know, the animal moves a bit, scares the guide, and I end up with a large African man sitting on my lap.

It turns out the cheetah was just looking for some shade and a little rest after a hunt. He didn't want to eat us – just use our vehicle for shade. As our guide kept reminding us, the Serengeti is not a zoo. It's a wild adventure where anything can happen. He was telling us that three people were killed while on safari last year. There is real danger while on safari.

In the two minutes that the cheetah was in our jeep, there was some fear but more curiosity, awe, and a desire to protect my family; however, every time I watch the video,[1] I get more and more scared about what could have happened, and at the same time feel a tension that I am scared but grateful for this incredible wildlife encounter that so few people get to experience! Tension is good. We can live in that tension.

The word "safari" has Swahili and Arabic roots, and it means journey. It has come to be understood as a big game hunt, and for some it produces an image of khaki-clad tourists with huge cameras around their necks – but the origin of the word is journey. While in contrast, the word "zoo" is short for zoological park, which is defined as a place to study captive animals.

I wonder if we treat our relationship with God more like a zoo than a safari. There is a lot to learn and appreciate at a zoo. In a zoo, there is clear protection with boundaries. There are clear expectations. Do not misunderstand me – zoos are fun – but zoos are designed to be safe.

C.S. Lewis describes the lion Aslan in the Narnia books as not tame – but good.[2] We serve a God who is not tame – He's wild beyond our wildest dreams! And if there is one thing that you need to know about growing and going and finding your identity, mission, and purpose in Jesus, it's that safety is not guaranteed! Following Jesus is an unpredictable adventure, and you never know what will happen next! But as with any great journey, it starts with the first step.

In years of teaching the C.S.I. model of Corporate Worship, Small Group, and Individual, perhaps the most common question I am asked is: "Does C.S.I. list the elements in order of importance?" Great question! No. They are not listed in order of importance, they are listed in order of size: big, small, one. I truly believe that in order to holistically understand our life in Jesus, all three areas need to be activated.

That being said, if I am pushed hard enough to give a crystal-clear answer on where to start (and since you made it to the end of the book, you deserve a crystal-clear answer on where to start!), here it is: S – Small Group. Specifically, I encourage starting with an accountability partner.

Does that surprise you? I find it does for many people, as they assume I will say "Go to church" as the first step. Going to church is certainly a good and logical answer. Yet, if we can find the right accountability partner, they will hold us accountable to find the right corporate worship setting, small group opportunity, and lovingly quiz us on our individual time with Jesus. That right person will remind us of the power of prayer as they pray with us, and they will encourage us to internalize the Word.

Can you find the right accountability partner? Here are a few tips on that. It's usually not your best friend. It's absolutely not your boyfriend/girlfriend. It's also a good idea to find someone besides your spouse – even though your spouse is certainly an accountability partner in many ways. Same gender is often best. Similar life experience can be helpful. While there is not a perfect way to find or chose an accountability partner, be sure to find someone who is trustworthy, loyal, and who will be honest with you and vice versa. You may actually want to find someone who has had a very different life experience than you, because they might be able to provide an insight that someone who's "like you" could never provide!

As much as we have focused on trinities in this book, there is something equally powerful about twos. Jesus sent out His followers two by two (Mark 6:7). St. Paul didn't go on any of his missionary journeys alone. As far as we know, he always had at least one companion. Perhaps you are being sent out two by two as well.

Of course, do not forget that after the first step of the journey comes the second, then the third, then the fourth, and so on. Meaning, it's one thing to start a journey, but a whole different thing to keep *going* and *growing* on that journey. The journey of following Jesus is a lifetime lifestyle of growing and going!

As you start this journey, I encourage you to pray about who that accountability partner might be. I have no doubt that God will use that person to help you become a Missionary Disciple, and to discover your identity, mission, and purpose in Jesus! Consider your accountability partner to be your safari guide, present with you on the journey – and lovingly reminding you that this is not a zoo!

May God bless you as you go forward in heart, mind, and soul to discover all He has in store for you through corporate worship, small groups, and your individual time with Him!

So – is *The Missionary Disciple* a redundant title for you? I hope and pray it is!

Dr. Jacob Youmans
Brief Autobiography

I'm a "nomad" who had never lived in the same house for more than five years, until we grew some roots in Texas over a decade ago. Both of my parents are Lutheran church workers, and we've moved around the country from adventure to adventure.

I was born in Winona, Minnesota, and then at the ripe old age of two moved to Richfield, Minnesota, outside of the Twin Cities. Later we packed up and moved to Cleveland, Ohio. After five years in Cleveland, and five losing seasons for the Cleveland Indians, we moved to Van Nuys, California, eventually settling into Sepulveda, CA. I had one year of high school at Los Angeles Lutheran High, then completed the next three in Las Vegas, Nevada.

After high school, I headed off to Concordia University in Irvine, California, and graduated in 1997 with a degree in Religious Studies. In 2003, I finished my Masters degree in Family Life Ministry at Concordia University Seward, Nebraska. And in 2008, I finished a doctoral program in Leadership in the Emerging Culture through George Fox University in Portland, Oregon. And the funny thing is that I stopped going to school just in time for my oldest daughter to start Kindergarten. Ah, the circle of life!

April 8th, 1997 was one of the most important days in my life. On that day I found out my DCE internship would be at Our Savior Lutheran Church in Aiea, Hawaii, and on that day I decided to ask my college sweetheart, Christy Lemon, to spend the rest of her life with me... How could she say no? We were moving to Hawaii! Christy is an artist and a musician. So without sounding too cheesy – and with me being color blind – she literally does complete me! People can tell when she hasn't picked out my clothes for me!

We were married June 20th, 1998. After four amazing years in Hawaii, we felt the Holy Spirit moving us to St. Paul's Lutheran Church in Orange, California. We are living proof there is a God, because no one leaves Hawaii unless God tells them to! I served as the High School Youth Minister and Family Minister during our eight years at St. Paul's. Also during that time, our family doubled in size with the addition of Maile Ann in 2003 and Leilani Mei in 2004. Back-to-back tax breaks! But I am now hopelessly outnumbered by females in my house.

In 2009, I started serving as a college professor and the Director of the DCE (Director of Christian Education) Program at Concordia University Texas in Austin. The move from the parish to higher education has been a good one, but a very different one. I absolutely loved my time in serving the local church, but I am excited and honored to be training future ministers, and I love placing them all over the world!

My passions in ministry are helping people realize and use their gifts and find creative ways to share the love of Jesus. I have been blessed enough to serve on mission trips on every continent except Antarctica! I love speaking and writing. It is such a privilege to bring God's love and hope in an energetic way. It's humbling to be on stage, but I cherish the opportunity to glorify God in that way. For speaking engagements, feel free to email me directly at Jacob.Youmans@Concordia.edu.

Endnotes & Additional Resources

Foreword by Dr. Grant Carey
[1] Andrew Byers, *Faith Without Illusions: Following Jesus as a Cynic-Saint* (Downers Grove, IL: Intervarsity Press, 2011), 63-64

How to Use This Book
[1] Michael S. Wilder and Shane W. Parker, *TransforMission: Making Disciples Through Short-Term Missions* (Nashville, TN: B&H Academic, 2010), 233

Chapter 1 – The Identity Questions

Who Are You?
[1] *Alice in Wonderland*. Dir. Clyde Geronimi, Wilfred Jackson and Hamilton Luske. Perf. Kathryn Beaumont, Ed Wynn, and Richard Hadyn. Walt Disney Productions, 1951, https://www.imdb.com/title/tt0043274/
[2] Neil Cole, *Organic Church: Growing Faith Where Life Happens* (San Francisco: Jossey-Bass, 2005), xxvii
[3] Wikipedia contributors. (2019, May 24). CSI (franchise). In *Wikipedia, The Free Encyclopedia*. Retrieved 01:51, June 10, 2019, from https://en.wikipedia.org/w/index.php?title=CSI_(franchise)&oldid=898639092
[4] The Who. "Who Are You." Who Are You, Ramport Studios, 1978, track 1. *Genius*, genius.com/The-who-who-are-you-lyrics.
[5] *Anger Management*. Dir. Peter Segal. Perf. Adam Sandler, Jack Nicholson, Marisa Tomei, and Luis Guzman. Revolution Studios, 2003, https://www.imdb.com/title/tt0305224/characters/nm0001191

Imagine Your Image
[1] Eugene Peterson, *The Message Full Size: The Bible in Contemporary Language* (Colorado Springs, CO: NavPress, 2014)
[2] Wong, K. (2014, September). The 1 Percent Difference. *Scientific American*, 100
[3] Eugene Peterson, *The Message Full Size: The Bible in Contemporary Language* (Colorado Springs, CO: NavPress, 2014)
[4] Galéra, C., Orriols, L., M'Bailara, K., Laborey, M., Contrand, B., Ribéreau-Gayon, R., … Lagarde, E. (2012). Mind wandering and

driving: responsibility case-control study. *BMJ (Clinical research ed.), 345*, e8105. doi:10.1136/bmj.e8105
5. Dietrich Bonhoeffer, *Life Together: The Classic Exploration of Christian Community*, tr. Doberstein (New York: Harper & Row, 1954), 77

Chapter 2 – C: Corporate Worship

Who's Who in Worship

1. Paraphrased from "Interview with Meet the Press," (PDF) transcript dated April 17, 1960, *Stanford University – The Martin Luther King Jr. Research and Education Institute*, http://okra.stanford.edu/transcription/document_images/Vol05Scans/17Apr1960_InterviewonMeetthePress.pdf
2. Neil Cole, *Organic Church: Growing Faith Where Life Happens* (San Francisco: Jossey-Bass, 2005), 39

Jesus Was No Pew Potato!

1. Darrell L. Bock, *Luke (IVP New Testament Commentary Series, Book 3)* (Downers Grove, IL: IVP Academic, 1994), 88

Ideas for You to Investigate

Finding Your Sanctuary

1. Kara Powell, "Doubt: A Faith Catastrophe or Catalyst?" *Proverbs 31 Ministries*, March 5, 2019, https://www.proverbs31.org/read/devotions/full-post/2019/03/05/doubt-a-faith-catastrophe-or-catalyst

Come and See!

1. Andrew F. Walls, *The Cross-Cultural Process in Christian History: Studies in the Transmission and Appropriation of Faith* (Maryknoll, New York: Orbis Books, 2002), 10

The Sacred Experienced

1. "Luther on Baptism," *The 7 Habits of Jesus*, April 10, 2015, http://www.7habitsofjesus.com/blog/luther-on-baptism
2. Joe Iovino, "5 Ways to Remember Your Baptism," *UMC.org*, September 1, 2017, http://www.umc.org/what-we-believe/5-ways-to-remember-your-baptism
3. For information on the Passover celebration see: http://jewishfederation.org/images/uploads/holiday_images/39497.pdf

Endnotes & Additional Resources

Chapter 3 – S: Small Group

Good Things Come in Small Packages
1. Thompson, John W. and Scruggs, Randy. "Sanctuary." Full Armor Publishing Company, 1982. *Genius*, https://genius.com/Maranatha-music-sanctuary-lyrics
2. For the current world population see: http://www.worldometers.info/world-population/

Ideas for You to Investigate

Gather Around the Word!
1. Free commentaries can be found at Bible Gateway: www.biblegateway.com

Serving Side by Side
1. Jacob Youmans, *Missional U: Life as a Mission Trip* (Anaheim Hills, CA: Tri-Pillar Publishing, 2013)
2. Jacob Youmans, *Missional Too: The Trip of a Lifetime* (Anaheim Hills, CA: Tri-Pillar Publishing, 2013)

Stronger Together
1. Wikipedia contributors. (2019, January 6). List of twelve-step groups. In *Wikipedia, The Free Encyclopedia*. Retrieved 19:14, June 9, 2019, from https://en.wikipedia.org/w/index.php?title=List_of_twelve-step_groups&oldid=877147343
2. Jonathan K. Dodson, *Fight Clubs: Gospel-Centered Discipleship* (The Resurgence, 2009)
3. Thomas Oppong, "This is How to Increase the Odds of Reaching Your Goals by 95%," *The Mission*, January 16, 2017, https://medium.com/the-mission/the-accountability-effect-a-simple-way-to-achieve-your-goals-and-boost-your-performance-8a07c76ef53a
4. Laura Vanderkam, "What You Need To Know To Create An Accountability Group That Works," *Fast Company*, January 22, 2014, https://www.fastcompany.com/3025193/what-you-need-to-know-to-create-an-accountability-group-that-works

Partners in Prayer
1. Ron Edmondson, "How My Personal Prayer Team Is Structured," *ChurchLeaders*, January 28, 2018, https://churchleaders.com/pastors/pastor-articles/161414-ron_edmondson_how_my_personal_prayer_team_is_structured.html

Chapter 4 – I: Individual

All by Myself... with Jesus
1. Andrew Haslam, "Luther's Advice: Concentrate When You Pray," *ThinkTheology*, September 10, 2015, https://thinktheology.co.uk/blog/article/luthers_advice_concentrate_when_you_pray

Keep Watch!
1. Andy Stanley, *Making Vision Stick* (Grand Rapids, MI: Zondervan, 2007), 61-62

How's Your Spiritual Health?
1. Roger Abrantes, "Live as If You Were to Die Tomorrow – Learn as If You Were to Live Forever," *Ethology Institute*, June 1, 2014, https://ethology.eu/live-as-if-you-were-to-die-tomorrow-learn-as-if-you-were-to-live-forever/
2. Billy Hung, "False Confucius Quotes," *While On Board*, April 3, 2017, https://whileonboard.wordpress.com/2017/04/03/false-confucius-quotes/
3. A.J. Swoboda, *Subversive Sabbath: The Surprising Power of Rest in a Nonstop World* (Grand Rapids, MI: Brazos Press, A Division of Baker Publishing Group, 2018), 15

Ideas for You to Investigate

Eating the Scroll
1. "Bible in a Year: 365-Day Reading Plan," *Biblica*, https://www.biblica.com/resources/reading-plans/
2. Martin Luther, "Preface to the Proverbs of Solomon," in *Word and Sacrament I*, ed. E. Theodore Bachmann, vol. 35 of *Luther's Works*, ed. Jaroslav Pelikan and Helmut T. Lehmann (Philadelphia: Fortress Press, 1960), 258
3. Bible Gateway, https://www.biblegateway.com/
4. For a dramatic reading presentation of the Gospel of Mark available on DVD, check out: https://www.csl.edu/resources/gospel-of-mark/

Writing Loudly
1. St. Augustine (author), Henry Chadwick (translator), *Confessions* (New York: Oxford University Press, 1998), 221
2. Leigh Ann Dutton, "How I Set up My New Prayer Journal," *Intentional by Grace*, March 17, 2016, https://intentionalbygrace.com/how-i-set-up-my-new-prayer-journal/

Go Away!
[1] Research actually suggests that boredom might be beneficial for us! For more information on this, see: Manoush Zomorodi, *Bored and Brilliant: How Spacing Out Can Unlock Your Most Productive and Creative Self* (New York: St. Martin's Press, 2017).

There is even a bored and brilliant challenge that can help you be bored: "Bored and Brilliant," *WNYC*, February 1-6, 2015, https://www.wnyc.org/series/bored-and-brilliant

Chapter 5 – Going as We're Growing
[1] *Avengers: Endgame*. Dir. Anthony Russo, Joe Russo. Perf. Robert Downey Jr., Chris Evans, Mark Ruffalo. Marvel Studios, 2019, https://www.imdb.com/title/tt4154796/?ref_=nv_sr_1?ref_=nv_sr_1
[2] Jacob Youmans, *Missional U: Life as a Mission Trip* (Anaheim Hills, CA: Tri-Pillar Publishing, 2013), 24-29

Chapter 6 – Not a Tame God
[1] You can see the video at: http://www.dailymail.co.uk/news/article-6058241/Cheetah-sits-open-sun-roof-poses-incredible-safari-photo.html
[2] Regarding Aslan, C.S. Lewis writes, "Who said anything about safe? 'Course he isn't safe. But he's good." C.S. Lewis, *The Lion, the Witch, and the Wardrobe* (New York: HarperCollins, 1978), 86

**Other books
by Dr. Jacob Youmans**

Life As a Mission Trip

Dr. Jacob Youmans

Missional Living 101!

Trips to the mission field always bring new spiritual growth and insight to our lives. What if we could learn to see mission not as an event to take part in, but as a lifestyle to embrace? In *Missional U: Life As a Mission Trip*, that's exactly what Dr. Jacob Youmans teaches us as he shows, through Scripture and by personal example, what missional living is all about! If you're looking for a new way to travel, then come along. Missional U is your ticket to an exciting and fulfilling spiritual adventure – one that's sure to last a lifetime!

Dr. Jacob Youmans, a dynamic conference speaker, is Director of the DCE Program at Concordia University in Austin, Texas.

$14.95 – Order online at ww.tripillarpublishing.com

MISSIONAL TOO

The Trip of a Lifetime

Dr. Jacob Youmans

Bon Voyage... Again!

In this second volume of devotions on the joy of missional living, Dr. Jacob Youmans shows us what it means to see the world through redemptive eyes, love the world with an evangelistic heart, and travel the world with the Gospel of peace firmly on our feet. In *Missional Too: The Trip of a Lifetime*, we discover that when we walk in the footsteps of Jesus, the imprint we leave behind is His, not our own – and that makes all the difference. Our journey here as God's dearly loved people is a Gospel-sharing, disciple-making one.

Dr. Jacob Youmans, a dynamic conference speaker, is Director of the DCE Program at Concordia University in Austin, Texas.

$14.95 – Order online at ww.tripillarpublishing.com

Abba Daddy Do

exploration s   in   child like   faith

by Dr. Jacob Youmans

Join the adventure of childlike faith!

When you're a child, every day is an adventure! Each day you see and experience life for the very first time. Reclaim the wonder and excitement meant for followers of Jesus as we explore the gift of childlike faith. Jacob Youmans, father of two, walks us through 40 true-life stories, discovering the spiritual in the everyday moments of childhood. Complete with study questions and scriptural references, this book is perfect for the individual looking to grow and be challenged, as well as a family or Bible study group.

Dr. Jacob Youmans, a dynamic conference speaker, is Director of the DCE Program at Concordia University in Austin, Texas.

$14.95 – Order online at ww.tripillarpublishing.com

Talking Pictures
How to turn a trip to the movies into a mission trip

by Dr. Jacob Youmans
Foreword by Leonard Sweet

Movies and ministry? What's the story?

Movies are everywhere - at the theater, at home, on our computers, even in our pockets! Our culture's fascination with the power of movies brings us together in a shared experience. But did you ever think that watching the latest action-adventure flick with a friend could provide a truly unique opportunity to witness about your Christian faith? Talking Pictures examines the power of movies in our culture and explores effective ways in which we can use any movie as a way to start conversations about our Christian faith.

Dr. Jacob Youmans, a dynamic conference speaker, is Director of the DCE Program at Concordia University in Austin, Texas.

$14.95 – Order online at ww.tripillarpublishing.com

Also from Tri-Pillar Publishing

Word Alive!
52 Selected Sermons by Dale A. Meyer
Dale A. Meyer

Timely Reflections:
A Minute a Day with Dale Meyer
Dale A. Meyer

Meeting Ananias
and Other Eye-Opening Stories of Faith
James Tino

Shaking Scripture:
Grasping More of God's Word
Mark Manning

Powerful Love: An Introduction to Christianity
Lloyd Strelow

Extraordinary News for Ordinary People
Heath Trampe

Order online at www.tripillarpublishing.com!

I'd love to hear how you're doing on your journey as a Missionary Disciple! Please feel free to drop me a line at Jacob.Youmans@Concordia.edu. I know God is going to use you in extraordinary ways to advance His kingdom! Know that I am praying for you, and I encourage you to be praying for all Missionary Disciples – around the world and in your backyard! God's richest blessings!

Mailing Address:
    Dr. Jacob Youmans
    Director, DCE Program
    Assistant Professor of Education
    Concordia-Texas
    11400 Concordia University Drive
    Austin, TX 78726

www.ingramcontent.com/pod-product-compliance
Lightning Source LLC
LaVergne TN
LVHW051835080426
835512LV00018B/2885